HANDBOOK OF
INAESTHETICS

MERIDIAN

Crossing Aesthetics

Werner Hamacher

Editor

Translated by
Alberto Toscano

Stanford
University
Press

Stanford
California

HANDBOOK OF
INAESTHETICS

Alain Badiou

Stanford University Press
Stanford, California

Handbook of Inaesthetics was originally published in French in
1998 under the title *Petit manuel d'inesthetique* © Editions du
Seuil, 1998.

This work, published as part of a program of aid for publica-
tion, received support from the French Ministry of Foreign
Affairs and the Cultural Services of the French Embassy in
the United States.

This book has been published with the assistance of the
French Ministry of Culture—National Center for the Book.

Printed in the United States of America
on acid-free, archival-quality paper

Library of Congress Cataloging-in-Publication Data

Badiou, Alain.
   [Petit manuel d'inesthetique. English]
   Handbook of inaesthetics / Alain Badiou, Alberto Toscano.
      p.   cm. — (Meridian)
   ISBN 0-8047-4408-4 (cloth : alk. paper)
   ISBN 0-8047-4409-2 (pbk. : alk. paper)
   1. Aesthetics.   I. Toscano, Alberto.   II. Title.
III. Meridian (Stanford, Calif.)
B2430.B273P3813 2004
111'.85—DC22

                                          2004001627

Original Printing 2005

Last figure below indicates year of this printing:
14   13   12   11   10   09   08   07   06

Contents

Translator's Note

Although I have tried to keep editorial interference with the text to a minimum—barring a handful of explanatory notes and indications of other works by Badiou, where concepts found in the *Handbook of Inaesthetics* are given their proper doctrinal formulations—the last two chapters of this book posed significant challenges that deserve brief elucidation.

Chapter 9, "Being, Existence, Thought: Prose and Concept," is a systematic reading, at once bold and meticulous, of Samuel Beckett's late prose text *Worstward Ho*, reconfigured here as a short treatise on ontology. The translation proved particularly arduous because, unlike most of Beckett's English prose, *Worstward Ho* was not translated into French by Beckett himself, and, moreover, what Badiou does with Beckett's text is overtly dependent on the abstractive capacity of Édith Fournier's translation and essentially pays no heed to the original text. It almost goes without saying that by inverting the direction of Badiou's operation, my translation of Badiou's essay has had to confront a number of serious challenges, often forcing me to test the resources of the English language in order to maintain the closeness of Badiou's reading and to accommodate the unique manner in which Beckett's own terminology is progressively appropriated into Badiou's prose. I hope that the distance produced by Badiou's having employed Fournier's translation will prove illuminating, even when the discussion of *Cap au pire* is translated into English and the citations are now from Beckett's original English version.

Chapter 10, "Philosophy of the Faun," is another "monograph" on in-aesthetics, in this instance concerned with one of Stéphane Mallarmé's most famous "Symbolist" poems, *L'après-midi d'un faune*. In order to maintain the consistency and indexicality of Badiou's commentary, I have been obliged to produce my own version of the poem, which is here quoted in its entirety. Far from claiming to having sought any poetic superiority over previous translations, I have simply aimed to maintain, to the best of my ability, the speculative armature identified in Badiou's discussion while simultaneously endeavoring not to inflict too much harm upon Mallarmé's language, and above all upon his syntax, which Badiou isolates as the crucial operator in the French poet's practice and thought. My effort here is deeply indebted to the translations by C. F. MacIntyre and Henry Weinfield and could in a sense be regarded as an amended hybrid of the two.[1]

Illegitimate as it may at first appear, I would maintain that such a "literalization," together with the perilous "return" of *Cap au pire* to its English original, is entirely consonant with the claims of Badiou's philosophy in general and registers one of the most obvious effects of inaesthetic discourse. Rather than seeking to welcome (that is, to absorb) the poem into the realm of speculative thinking in a hermeneutic vein, Badiou's approach is committed both to declaring the autonomy of artistic procedures (poetic or literary, cinematic or theatrical) and to registering what he calls their "intraphilosophical effects." (See the epigraph to this volume.) It is worth noting in this respect that the practice of translation, while constituting "an almost invariably disastrous approximation" (Chapter 5 below), nevertheless functions—as Badiou himself avows with specific reference to Beckett—as a potent weapon in the arsenal of inaesthetics, preparing the extraction from the works in question of those traits that single them out as conditions for philosophical activity. In his own "flattening or punctuation" of Mallarmé's poems, aimed at discerning their "syntactical becoming"—what he in effect dubs their "translation"—Badiou concisely defines this operation as one in which "the poem is withdrawn from all poetry."[2] It is in line with such a "withdrawal" that I have opted for the consistency of reference and syntax over that of rhyme and in accordance with which I have modified some translations whose "poetry" is surely superior to my own.

The original text, in accordance with Badiou's customary practice, is devoid of references. All endnotes are my own. Following the reasons adduced by Daniel W. Smith in his translation of Deleuze's "Desire and Pleasure," I have chosen to leave *dispositif* in the French.

I would like to express my profound gratitude to Nina Power and Roberto Toscano for reading through drafts of this translation and kindly sparing me some grievous errors and omissions, to Bud Bynack for his meticulous and insightful editorial comments, to John Felstiner for generously providing the two new translations of Paul Celan in Chapter 3, to Ray Brassier and Peter Hallward for their suggestions and their indispensable contribution to my understanding of Badiou's thought, and, finally, to Alain Badiou, for his assistance, friendship, and abiding support.

HANDBOOK OF
INAESTHETICS

By "inaesthetics" I understand a relation of philosophy to art that, maintaining that art is itself a producer of truths, makes no claim to turn art into an object for philosophy. Against aesthetic speculation, inaesthetics describes the strictly intraphilosophical effects produced by the independent existence of some works of art.

    —A. B., April 1998

§ 1 Art and Philosophy

This link has always been affected by a symptom—that of an oscillation or a pulse.

At its origins there lies the judgment of ostracism that Plato directed against poetry, theater, and music. We must face the fact that in the *Republic,* the founder of philosophy, clearly a refined connoisseur of all the arts of his time, spares only military music and patriotic song.

At the other extreme, we find a pious devotion to art, a contrite prostration of the concept—regarded as a manifestation of technical nihilism—before the poetic word, which is alone in offering the world up to the latent Openness of its own distress.[1]

But, after all, it is already with the sophist Protagoras that we encounter the designation of artistic apprenticeship as the key to education. An alliance existed between Protagoras and Simonides the poet—a subterfuge that Plato's Socrates tried to thwart, so as to submit its thinkable intensity to his own ends.

An image comes to mind, an analogical matrix of meaning: Historically, philosophy and art are paired up like Lacan's Master and Hysteric. We know that the hysteric comes to the master and says: "Truth speaks through my mouth, I am *here*. You have knowledge, tell me who I am." Whatever the knowing subtlety of the master's reply, we can also anticipate that the hysteric will let him know that it's not yet *it*, that her *here* escapes the master's grasp, that it must all be taken up again and worked through at length in order to please her. In so doing, the hysteric takes charge of the master, "barring" him from mastery and becoming his mistress.[2] Likewise, art is always already there, addressing the thinker with the

mute and scintillating question of its identity while through constant invention and metamorphosis it declares its disappointment about everything that the philosopher may have to say about it.

If he balks at amorous servitude and at the idolatry that represents the
price of this exhausting and ever deceptive production of knowledge, the
hysteric's master hardly has another choice than to give her a good beat-
ing.[3] Likewise, the philosopher-master remains divided, when it comes to
art, between idolatry and censure. Either he will say to the young (his dis-
ciples) that at the heart of every virile education of reason lies the imperative of holding oneself at a remove from the Creature, or he will end up
conceding that she alone—this opaque brilliance that cannot but hold us
captive—instructs us about the angle from which truth commands the
production of knowledge.

And since what we are required to elucidate is the link between art and
philosophy, it seems that, formally speaking, this link is thought in accordance with two schemata.

The first is what I will call the *didactic* schema. Its thesis is that art is incapable of truth, or that all truth is external to art. This thesis will certainly acknowledge that art presents itself (like the hysteric) in the guise of
effective, immediate, or naked truth. Moreover, it will suggest that this
nakedness exposes art as the pure *charm* of truth. More precisely, it will
say that art is the appearance of an unfounded or nondiscursive truth, of
a truth that is exhausted in its being-there. But—and this is the whole
point of the Platonic trial—this pretence or seduction will be rejected.
The heart of the Platonic polemic about mimesis designates art not so
much as an imitation of things, but as the imitation of the effect of truth.
This is an imitation that draws its power from its *immediate* character.
Plato will therefore argue that to be the prisoners of an immediate image
of truth *diverts us from the detour*. If truth can exist as charm, then we are
fated to lose the force of dialectical labor, of the slow argumentation that
prepares the way for the ascent to the Principle. We must therefore de-
nounce the supposedly immediate truth of art as a false truth, as the semblance that belongs to the effect of truth. The definition of art, and of art
alone, is thus the following: To be the charm of a semblance of truth.

It follows that art must be either condemned or treated in a purely in-
strumental fashion. Placed under strict surveillance, art lends the transitory force of semblance or of charm to a truth that is prescribed *from outside*. Acceptable art must be subjected to the philosophical surveillance of

truths. This position upholds a didactics of the senses whose aim cannot be abandoned to immanence. The norm of art must be education; the norm of education is philosophy. This is the first knot that ties our three terms (art, philosophy, and education) together.

In this perspective, the essential thing is the control of art. This control is possible. Why? Because if the truth of which art is capable comes to it from outside—if art is a didactics of the senses—it follows, and this point is crucial, that the "good" essence of art is conveyed in its public effect, and not in the artwork itself. As Rousseau writes in the *Letter to D'Alembert*: "The spectacle is made for the people, and it is only by its effects upon the people that its absolute qualities can be determined."

In the didactic schema, the absolute of art is thus controlled by the public effects of semblance, effects that are in turn regulated by an extrinsic truth.

This educational injunction is itself absolutely opposed by what I will call the *romantic* schema. Its thesis is that art *alone* is capable of truth. What's more, it is in this sense that art accomplishes what philosophy itself can only point toward. In the romantic schema, art is the real body of truth, or what Lacoue-Labarthe and Nancy have named "the literary absolute." It is patent that this real body is a glorious body. Philosophy might very well be the withdrawn and impenetrable Father—art is the suffering Son who saves and redeems. Genius is crucifixion and resurrection. In this respect, it is art itself that educates, because it teaches of the power of infinity held within the tormented cohesion of a form. Art delivers us from the subjective barrenness of the concept. Art is the absolute as subject—it is *incarnation.*

Nevertheless, between didactic banishment and romantic glorification (a "between" that is not essentially temporal) there is—it seems—an age of relative peace between art and philosophy. The question of art does not torment Descartes, Leibniz, or Spinoza. It appears that these great classical thinkers do not have to choose between the severity of control and the ecstasy of allegiance.

Was it not Aristotle himself who had already signed, between art and philosophy, a peace treaty of sorts? All the evidence points to the existence of a third schema, the *classical* schema, of which one will say from the start that it *dehystericizes art.*

The classical *dispositif,* as constructed by Aristotle, is contained in two theses:

a) Art—as the didactic schema argues—is incapable of truth. Its essence is mimetic, and its regime is that of semblance.

b) This incapacity does not pose a serious problem (contrary to what Plato believed). This is because the *purpose* [*destination*] of art is not in the least truth. Of course, art is not truth, but it also does not claim to be truth and is therefore innocent. Aristotle's prescription places art under the sign of something entirely other than knowledge and thereby frees it from the Platonic suspicion. This other thing, which he sometimes names "catharsis," involves the deposition of the passions in a transference onto semblance. Art has a therapeutic function, and not at all a cognitive or revelatory one. Art does not pertain to the theoretical, but to the ethical (in the widest possible sense of the term). It follows that the norm of art is to be found in its utility for the treatment of the affections of the soul.

The great rules concerning art can be immediately inferred from the two theses of the classical schema.

The criterion of art is first of all that of liking. In no respect is "liking" a rule of opinion, a rule of the greatest number. Art must be liked because "liking" signals the effectiveness of catharsis, the real grip exerted by the artistic therapy of the passions.

Second, the name of what "liking" relates to is not truth. "Liking" is bound only to what extracts from a truth the arrangement of an identification. The "resemblance" to the true is required only to the degree that it engages the spectator of art in "liking," that is, in an identification that organizes a transference and thus in a deposition of the passions. This scrap of truth is therefore not truth per se, but rather what *a truth constrains within the imaginary*. This "imaginarization" of truth, which is relieved of any instance of the Real, is what the classical thinkers called "verisimilitude" or "likelihood."

In the end, the peace between philosophy and art rests entirely on the demarcation of truth from verisimilitude. This is why the classical maxim par excellence is: "The true is sometimes not the likely." This maxim states the demarcation and maintains—*beside* art—the rights of philosophy. Philosophy, which clearly grants itself the possibility of being without verisimilitude. We encounter here a classical definition of philosophy: The unlikely truth.

What is the cost of this peace between philosophy and art? Without doubt, art is innocent, but this is because it is innocent of all truth. In other words, it is inscribed in the imaginary. Strictly speaking, within the classical schema, art is not a form of thought. It is entirely exhausted by its act or by its public operation. "Liking" turns art into a service. To summarize, we could say that in the classical view, art is a public service. After all, this is how it is understood by the state in the "vassalization" of art and artists by absolutism, as well as in the modern vicissitudes of funding. In terms of the link that preoccupies us here, the state is essentially classical (perhaps with the exception of the socialist state, which was rather didactic).

Let us briefly recapitulate our argument.

Didacticism, romanticism, and classicism are the possible schemata of the link between art and philosophy—the third term of this link being the education of subjects, the youth in particular. In didacticism, philosophy is tied to art in the modality of an educational surveillance of art's purpose, which views it as extrinsic to truth. In romanticism, art realizes within finitude all the subjective education of which the philosophical infinity of the idea is capable. In classicism, art captures desire and shapes [*éduque*] its transference by proposing a semblance of its object. Philosophy is summoned here only qua aesthetics: It has its say about the rules of "liking."

In my view, the century that is coming to a close was characterized by the fact that it did not introduce, on a massive scale, any new schema. Though it is considered to be the century of endings, breaks, and catastrophes, when it comes to the link that concerns us here, I see it instead as a century that was simultaneously conservative and eclectic.

What are the massive tendencies of thought in the twentieth century? Its massively identifiable *singularities*? I can see only three: Marxism, psychoanalysis, and German hermeneutics.

It is clear that as regards the thinking of art, Marxism is didactic, psychoanalysis classical, and Heideggerian hermeneutics romantic.

The proof that Marxism is didactic need not be located immediately in the evidence of the ukases and persecutions that were perpetrated in the socialist states. The surest proof lies in Brecht's unbridled creative thought. For Brecht, there exists a general and extrinsic truth, a truth the character of which is scientific. This truth is dialectical materialism, whose status as the solid base of the new rationality Brecht never cast into doubt. This truth is essentially philosophical, and the "philosopher" is the leading character in Brecht's didactic dialogues. It is the philosopher who is in charge of the surveillance of art through the latent supposition of a dialectical truth. It is in this respect that Brecht remained a Stalinist, if by Stalinism we understand—as indeed we should—the fusion of politics and of dialectical materialist philosophy under the jurisdiction of the latter. We could also say that Brecht practiced a Stalinized Platonism. Brecht's supreme goal was to create a "society of the friends of dialectics," and the theater was, in more than one respect, the instrument of such a society. The alienation effect is a protocol of philosophical surveillance *in actu* with regard to the educational ends of theater. Semblance must be alienated [*mis à distance*] from itself so as to *show*, in the gap thus formed, the extrinsic objectivity of the true.

Fundamentally, Brecht's greatness lay in having obstinately searched for the immanent rules of a Platonic (didactic) art, instead of remaining content, like Plato, with classifying the existing arts as either good or bad. His "non-Aristotelian" (meaning nonclassical and ultimately Platonic) theater is an artistic invention of the first caliber within the reflexive element of a subordination of art. Brecht theatrically reactivated Plato's antitheatrical measures. He did so by turning the possible forms of the subjectivation of an external truth into the focal point of art.

The importance of the epic dimension also originates in this program. The epic is what exhibits—in the interval of the performance—the *courage* of truth. For Brecht, art produces no truth, but is instead an elucidation—based on the supposition that the true exists—of the conditions for a courage of truth. Art, under surveillance, is a therapy against cowardice. Not against cowardice in general, but against cowardice *in the face of truth*. This is obviously why the figure of Galileo is central, and also why this play is Brecht's tormented masterpiece, the one in which the paradox of an epic that would be internal to the exteriority of truth turns upon itself.

It is evident, I think, that Heideggerian hermeneutics remains romantic. By all appearances, it exposes an indiscernible entanglement between the saying of the poet and the thought of the thinker. Nevertheless, the advantage is still with the poet, because the thinker is nothing but the announcement of a reversal, the promise of the advent of the gods at the height of our distress, and the retroactive elucidation of the historiality of being. While the poet, in the flesh of language, maintains the effaced guarding of the Open.

We could say that Heidegger unfolds the figure of the poet-thinker as the obverse of Nietzsche's philosopher-artist. But what interests us here and characterizes the romantic schema is that between philosophy and art it is *the same truth that circulates*. The retreat of being comes to thought in the conjoining of the poem and its interpretation. Interpretation is in the end nothing but the *delivery* of the poem over to the trembling of finitude in which thought strives to endure the retreat of being as clearing. Poet and thinker, relying on one another, embody within the word the opening out of its closure [*le déclos de sa cloture*]. In this respect, the poem, strictly speaking, cannot be equaled.

Psychoanalysis is Aristotelian, absolutely classical. In order to be persuaded of this, it suffices to read Freud's writings on painting and Lacan's pronouncements on the theater or poetry. In Freud and Lacan, art is conceived as what makes it so that the object of desire, which is beyond symbolization, can subtractively emerge at the very peak of an act of symbolization. In its formal bearing, the work leads to the dissipation of the unspeakable scintillation of the lost object. In so doing, it ineluctably captivates the gaze or the hearing of the one who is exposed to it. The work of art links up to a transference because it exhibits, in a singular and contorted configuration, the blockage of the symbolic by the Real, the "extimacy"[4] of the *objet petit a* (the cause of desire) to the Other (the treasure of the symbolic). This is why the ultimate effect of art remains imaginary.

I can therefore conclude as follows: This century, which essentially has not modified the doctrines concerning the link between art and philosophy, has nevertheless experienced the *saturation* of these doctrines. Didacticism is saturated by the state-bound and historical exercise of art in the service of the people. Romanticism is saturated by the element of pure promise—always brought back to the supposition of a return of the gods—in Heidegger's rhetorical equipment. Classicism, finally, is saturated by the self-consciousness conferred upon it by the complete deployment of a theory of desire. Whence, if one has not already fallen prey to the lures of an "applied psychoanalysis," the ruinous conviction that the relationship between psychoanalysis and art is never anything but a service rendered to psychoanalysis itself: Art as free service.

That today the three schemata are saturated tends to produce a kind of disentanglement of the terms, a desperate "disrelation" between art and philosophy, together with the pure and simple collapse of what had circulated between them: the pedagogical theme.

From Dadaism to Situationism, the century's avant-gardes have been nothing but escort experiments for contemporary art, and not the adequate designation of the real operations of this art. The role of the avant-gardes was to represent, rather than to link. This is because they were nothing but the desperate and unstable search for a mediating schema, for a didactico-romantic schema. The avant-gardes were didactic in their desire to put an end to art, in their condemnation of its alienated and inauthentic character. But they were also romantic in their conviction that art must be reborn immediately as absolute—as the undivided awareness of its operations or as its own immediately legible truth. Considered as the harbingers of a didactico-romantic schema or as the partisans of the absoluteness of creative destruction, the avant-gardes were above all anticlassical.

Their limit lay in their incapacity to place a lasting seal on their alliances, with respect either to the contemporary forms of the didactic schema or to those of the romantic one. In empirical terms: Just like the fascism of Marinetti and the Futurists, the communism of Breton and the Surrealists remained merely allegorical. The avant-gardes did not achieve their conscious objective: to lead a united front against classicism. Revolutionary didactics condemned them on the grounds of their romantic traits: the leftism of total destruction and of a self-consciousness fashioned ex nihilo, an incapacity for action on a grand scale, a fragmentation into small groups. Hermeneutic romanticism condemned them on the grounds of their didactic traits: an affinity for revolution, intellectualism, contempt for the state. Above all, it condemned them because the didacticism of the avant-gardes was marked by a brand of aesthetic voluntarism. And we know that, for Heidegger, the will constitutes the last subjective figure of contemporary nihilism.

Today, the avant-gardes have disappeared. The global situation is basically marked by two developments: on the one hand, the saturation of the three inherited schemata, on the other, the closure of every effect produced by the only schema that the century applied, which was in fact a synthetic schema: didacto-romanticism.

The thesis of which this book is but a series of variations can therefore be stated as follows: In this situation of saturation and closure, it is necessary to propose a new schema, a fourth modality of the link between philosophy and art.

The method of our inquiry will at first be negative: What do the three inherited schemata—didactic, romantic, classical—have in common, that today we would need to rid ourselves of? I believe that the "common" of these three schemata concerns the relation between art and truth.

The categories of this relation are immanence and singularity. "Immanence" refers to the following question: Is truth really internal to the artistic effect of works of art? Or is the artwork instead nothing but the instrument of an external truth? "Singularity" points us to another question: Does the truth testified by art belong to it absolutely? Or can this truth circulate among other registers of work-producing thought [*la pensée uvrante*]?

What can we immediately observe? First, that in the romantic schema, the relation of truth to art is indeed immanent (art exposes the finite descent of the Idea), but not singular (because we are dealing with *the* truth and the thinker's thought is not attuned to something different from what is unveiled in the saying of the poet). Second, that in didacticism, the relation is certainly singular (only art can exhibit a truth *in the form of semblance*), but not at all immanent, because the position of truth is ultimately extrinsic. And third, that in classicism, we are dealing only with the constraint that a truth exercises within the domain of the imaginary in the guise of verisimilitude, of the "likely."

In these inherited schemata, the relation between artworks and truth never succeeds in being at once singular and immanent.

We will therefore affirm this simultaneity. In other words: Art *itself* is a truth procedure. Or again: The philosophical identification of art falls under the category of truth. Art is a thought in which artworks are the Real (and not the effect). And this thought, or rather the truths that it activates, are irreducible to other truths—be they scientific, political, or amorous. This also means that art, as a singular regime of thought, is irreducible to philosophy.

Immanence: Art is rigorously coextensive with the truths that it generates.

Singularity: These truths are given nowhere else than in art.

According to this vision of things, what becomes of the third term of the link, the pedagogical function of art? Art is pedagogical for the simple reason that it produces truths and because "education" (save in its oppressive or perverted expressions) has never meant anything but this: to arrange the forms of knowledge in such a way that some truth may come to pierce a hole in them.

What art educates us for is therefore nothing apart from its own existence. The only question is that of *encountering* this existence, that is, of thinking through a form of thought [*penser une pensée*].

Philosophy's relation to art, like its relation to every other truth procedure, comes down to *showing* it as it is. Philosophy is the go-between in our encounters with truths, the procuress of truth. And just as beauty is to be found in the woman encountered, but is in no way required of the procuress, so it is that truths are artistic, scientific, amorous, or political, and not philosophical.

The problem is therefore concentrated upon the *singularity* of the artistic procedure, upon what authorizes its irreducible differentiation—vis-à-vis science or politics, for example.

It is imperative to recognize that beneath its manifest simplicity—its naiveté, even—the thesis according to which art would be a truth procedure sui generis, both immanent and singular, is in fact an absolutely novel philosophical proposition. Most of the consequences of this thesis remain veiled, and it demands from us a considerable labor of reformulation. The symptom of this novelty can be registered when we consider that Deleuze, for example, continues to place art on the side of sensation as such (percept and affect), in paradoxical continuity with the Hegelian motif of art as the "sensible form of the Idea." Deleuze thereby disjoins art from philosophy (which is devoted to the invention of concepts alone), in line with a modality of demarcation that still leaves the destination of art as a form of thought entirely unapparent. This is because if one fails to summon the category of truth in this affair, one cannot hope to succeed in establishing the plane of immanence from which the differentiation between art, science, and philosophy can proceed.

I think that the principal difficulty in this respect derives from the following point: When one undertakes the thinking of art as an immanent production of truths, *what is the pertinent unity of what is called "art"*? Is it the artwork itself, the singularity of a work? Is it the author, the creator? Or is it something else?

In actual fact, the essence of the question has to do with the problem of the relation between the infinite and the finite. A truth is an infinite multiplicity. I cannot establish this point here by way of formal demonstration, as I have done elsewhere.[5] Let us say that this was the insight proper to the partisans of the romantic schema, before they obliterated their discovery in the aesthetic diagram of finitude, of the artist as the Christ of the Idea. Or, to be more conceptual: The infinity of a truth is the property whereby it subtracts itself from its pure and simple identity with the established forms of knowledge.

A work of art is essentially finite. It is trebly finite. First of all, it exposes itself as finite objectivity in space and/or in time. Second, it is always regulated by a Greek principle of completion: It moves within the fulfillment of its own limit. It signals its display of all the perfection of which it is capable. Finally, and most importantly, it sets itself up as an inquiry into the question of its own finality. It is the persuasive procedure of its own finitude. This is, after all, why the artwork is irreplaceable in all of its points (another trait that distinguishes it from the generic infinite of the true): Once "left" to its own immanent ends, it is as it will forever be, and every touch-up or modification is either inessential or destructive.

I would even happily argue that the work of art is in fact the only finite thing that exists—that art creates finitude. Put otherwise, art is the creation of an intrinsically finite multiple, a multiple that exposes its own organization in and by the finite framing of its presentation and that turns this border into the stakes of its existence.

Thus, if one wishes to argue that the work is a truth, by the same token, one will also have to maintain that it is the descent of the infinite-true into finitude. But this figure of the descent of the infinite into the finite is precisely the kernel of the romantic schema that thinks art as incarnation. It is striking to see that this schema is still at work in Deleuze, for whom art entertains with the chaotic infinite the most faithful of relationships precisely because it configures the chaotic within the finite.

It does not appear that the desire to propose a schema of the art/philosophy link that would be neither classical, didactic, nor romantic is compatible with the retention of the work as the pertinent unit of inquiry—at least not if we wish to examine art under the sign of the truths of which it is capable.

All the more so given a supplementary difficulty: Every truth originates in an event. Once again, I leave this assertion in its axiomatic state. Let us say that it is vain to imagine that one could *invent* anything at all (and every truth is an invention) were nothing to happen, were "nothing to have taken place but the place." One would then be back at an "ingenious" or idealistic conception of invention. The problem that we need to deal with is that it is impossible to say of the work *at one and the same time* that it is a truth and that it is the event whence this truth originates. It is very often argued that the work of art must be thought of as an evental singularity, rather than as a structure. But every fusion of the event and truth returns us to a "Christly" vision of truth, because a truth is then nothing but its own evental self-revelation.

I think the path to be followed is encapsulated in a small number of propositions.

—As a general rule, a work is not an event. A work is a fact of art. It is the fabric from which the artistic procedure is woven.

—Nor is a work of art a truth. A truth is an artistic procedure initiated by an event. This procedure is *composed* of nothing but works. But it does not manifest itself (as infinity) in any of them. The work is thus the local instance or the differential point of a truth.

—We will call this differential point of the artistic procedure its *subject*. A work is the subject of the artistic procedure in question, that is, the procedure to which this work belongs. In other words: An artwork is a subject point of an artistic truth.

—The sole being of a truth is that of works. An artistic truth is a (infinite) generic multiple of works. But these works weave together the being of an artistic truth only by the chance of their successive occurrences.

—We can also say this: A work is a situated *inquiry* about the truth that it locally actualizes or of which it is a finite fragment.

—The work is thus submitted to a principle of novelty. This is because an inquiry is retroactively validated as a real work of art only inasmuch as it is an inquiry *that had not taken place*, an unprecedented subject-point within the trajectory of a truth.

—Works compose a truth within the post-evental dimension that institutes *the constraint of an artistic configuration*. In the end, a truth is an artistic configuration initiated by an event (in general, an event is a group of works, a singular multiple of works) and unfolded through chance in the form of the works that serve as its subject points.

In the final analysis, the pertinent unit for a thinking of art as an immanent and singular truth is thus neither the work nor the author, but rather the artistic configuration initiated by an eventual rupture (which in general renders a prior configuration obsolete). This configuration, which is a generic multiple, possesses neither a proper name nor a proper contour, not even a possible totalization in terms of a single predicate. It cannot be exhausted, only imperfectly described. It is an artistic truth, and everybody knows that there is no truth of truth. Finally, an artistic configuration is generally designated by means of abstract concepts (the figural, the tonal, the tragic...).

What are we to understand, more precisely, by "artistic configuration"?

A configuration is not an art form, a genre, or an "objective" period in the history of art, nor is it a "technical" *dispositif.* Rather, it is an identifiable sequence, initiated by an event, comprising a virtually infinite complex of works, when speaking of which it makes sense to say that it produces—in a rigorous immanence to the art in question—a truth *of this art*, an art-truth. Philosophy will bear the trace of this configuration inasmuch as it will have to show in what sense this configuration lets itself be grasped by the category of truth. The philosophical montage of the category of truth will in turn be singularized by the artistic configurations of its time. In this sense, it is true to say that, more often than not, a configuration is thinkable at the juncture of an effective process within art and of the philosophies that seize this process.

One will point to Greek tragedy, for example, which has been grasped as a configuration time and again, from Plato or Aristotle to Nietzsche. The initiating event of tragedy bears the name "Aeschylus," but this name, like every other name of an event, is really the index of a central void in the previous situation of choral poetry. We know that with Euripides, the configuration reaches its point of saturation. In music, rather than referring to the tonal system, which is far too structural a *dispositif,* one will refer to the "classical style" in the sense that Charles Rosen speaks of it, that is, as an identifiable sequence stretching out between Haydn and Beethoven. Likewise, one will doubtless say that—from Cervantes to Joyce—the novel is the name of a configuration for prose.

It will be noted that the saturation of a configuration (the narrative novel around the time of Joyce, the classical style around that of Beethoven, etc.) in no way signifies that said configuration is a finite multiplicity. Nothing from within the configuration itself either delimits it or exposes the principle of its end. The rarity of proper names and the brevity of the sequence are inconsequential empirical data. Besides, beyond the proper names retained as significant illustrations of the configuration or as the "dazzling" subject points of its generic trajectory, there is always a virtually infinite quantity of subject points—minor, ignored, redundant, and so on—that are no less a part of the immanent truth whose being is provided by the artistic configuration. Of course, it can happen that the configuration no longer gives rise to distinctly perceivable works or to decisive inquiries into its own constitution. It can also happen that an incalculable event comes to reveal in retrospect a configuration to be obsolete with respect to the constraints introduced by a new configuration. But in any case, unlike the works that constitute its material, a truth configuration is intrinsically infinite. This clearly means that the configuration ignores every internal maximum, every apex, and every peroration. After all, a configuration may always be seized upon again in epochs of uncertainty or rearticulated in the naming of a new event.

From the fact that the thinkable extraction of a configuration often takes place on the edges of philosophy—because philosophy is conditioned by art *as singular truth* and therefore by art as arranged into infinite configurations—we must above all not conclude that it is philosophy's task to think art. Instead, *a configuration thinks itself in the works that compose it.* Let's not forget that a work is an inventive inquiry into the configuration, which therefore thinks the thought that the configuration *will have been* (under the presumption of its infinite completion). To put it more precisely: The configuration thinks itself through the test posed by an inquiry that, at one and the same time, reconstructs it locally, sketches its "to come," and retroactively reflects its temporal arc. From this point of view, it is necessary to maintain that art—as the configuration "in truth" of works—is in each and every one of its points the thinking of the thought that it itself is [*pensée de la pensée qu'il est*].

We can therefore declare that we've inherited a threefold problem:

—What are the contemporary configurations of art?

—What becomes of philosophy as conditioned by art?

—What happens to the theme of education?

We will leave the first point alone. The whole of contemporary thinking about art is full of inquiries—often enthralling ones—about the artistic configurations that have marked the century: dodecaphonic music, novelistic prose, the age of poets, the rupture of the figurative, and so on.

On the second point, I cannot but reiterate my own convictions: Philosophy, or rather *a* philosophy, is always the elaboration of a category of truth. Philosophy does not itself produce any effective truth. It seizes truths, shows them, exposes them, announces that they exist. In so doing, it turns time toward eternity—since every truth, as a generic infinity, is eternal. Finally, philosophy makes disparate truths compossible and, on this basis, it states the being of the time in which it operates as the time of the truths that arise within it.

Concerning the third point, let us recall that the only education is an education *by* truths. The entire, insistent problem is that there be truths, without which the philosophical category of truth is entirely empty and the philosophical act nothing but an academic quibble.

This question of the existence of truths (that "there be" truths) points to a coresponsibility of art, which produces truths, and philosophy, which, under the condition that there are truths, is duty-bound to make them manifest (a very difficult task indeed). Basically, to make truths manifest means the following: to distinguish truths from opinion. So that the question today is this and no other: Is there something besides opinion? In other words (one will, or will not, forgive the provocation), is there something besides our "democracies"?

Many will answer, myself among them: "Yes." Yes, there are artistic configurations, there are works that constitute the thinking subjects of these configurations, and there is philosophy to separate conceptually all of this from opinion. Our times are worth more than the label on which they pride themselves: "democracy."

In order to nourish this conviction in the reader, we will therefore begin with some philosophical *identifications* of the arts. Poetry, theater, cinema, and dance will be our pretexts.

§ 2   What is a Poem?, Or, Philosophy and Poetry at the Point of the Unnamable

Does the radical critique of poetry in book 10 of the *Republic* manifest the singular limits of the Platonic philosophy of the Idea? Or is it, on the contrary, a constitutive gesture of philosophy "as such," which would thereby originally manifest its incompatibility with the poem?

To prevent the debate from becoming insipid, it is important to grasp that the Platonic gesture directed at the poem is, in Plato's own mind, neither ancillary nor polemical. This is a truly crucial point. Plato does not hesitate to declare the following: "We were entirely right in our organization of the city, and especially, I think, in the matter of poetry." [1]

It is absolutely necessary to keep intact the incisive character of this extraordinary statement. It tells us, without further ado, that the measure of political principle is precisely the exclusion of the poem. Or at least the exclusion of what Plato calls the "imitative dimension" of the poetic. The fate of true politics is staked on the firmness of its attitude toward the poem.

But what is true politics, the well-founded *politeia*? It is philosophy itself, to the extent that philosophy guarantees the grip of thought upon collective existence, upon the assembled multiplicity of men. We could say that *politeia* designates the collective that has attained its immanent truth. In other words, it designates the collective commensurable with thought.

If we are to follow Plato, we must therefore assert the following: The city, which is the name of assembled humanity, is thinkable only inasmuch as its concept is sheltered from the poem. If the city is to be exposed to thought, it is necessary to shelter subjective collectivity from the powerful charms of the poem. In other words, as long as it is "poeticized," collective subjectivity is also subtracted from thought and remains heterogeneous to it.

The usual interpretation—amply legitimated by Plato's text—is that the poem forbids any access to the supreme principle, the principle that allows the truth of the collective to achieve its own transparency. This is because the poem is situated at a twofold distance from the Idea, being but a secondary imitation of the primary imitation that the sensible constitutes. The protocol of the poets' banishment would therefore seem to depend upon the imitative nature of poetry. To prohibit poetry and to critique mimesis would thus amount to the same thing.

I do not think that this interpretation is a match for the *violence* of the Platonic text. This is a violence that Plato does not conceal, because it is also aimed at himself, directed against the irrepressible power that the poem holds over his own soul. The reasonable critique of imitation does not entirely legitimate the claim that one must wrest the effects of such power from oneself.

Suppose that mimesis is not the source of our problem, that it takes a fundamental misunderstanding to believe that in order to think the city it is necessary to interrupt—upstream from mimesis, as it were—poetic speech.

It seems that between thought such as philosophy thinks it, on the one hand, and the poem, on the other, there is a far more radical and far more ancient discord than the one regarding images and imitation.

It is this deep and ancient discord that I believe Plato alludes to when he writes: "palaia tis diaphora philosophia te kai poietike," "there is from old a quarrel between philosophy and poetry."[2]

The antiquity of this quarrel obviously bears on thought, on the identification of thought.

To what, within thought, is poetry opposed? Poetry is not directly opposed to the intellect (*nous*), to the intuition of ideas. It is not opposed to dialectics, considered as the supreme form of the intelligible. Plato is very clear on this point: What poetry forbids is discursive thought, *dianoia*. Plato says that "he who lends an ear to it must be on his guard fearing for the polity in his soul."[3] *Dianoia* is the thought that traverses, the thought that links and deduces. The poem itself is affirmation and delectation—it does not traverse, it dwells on the threshold. The poem is not a rule-bound crossing, but rather an offering, a lawless proposition.

Plato will also say that the genuine resort against the poem is to be sought in "measure, number, and weight." Moreover, the antipoetic part of the soul is defined as "the labor of calculating *logos*," "ton logistikon ergon." Plato will also remark that what triumphs in the theatrical poem is the principle of pleasure and pain, against both the law and the *logos*.

Dianoia, the thought that links and traverses, the thought that is a *logos* subject to a law, has a paradigm. This paradigm is mathematics. We can therefore argue that what the poem is opposed to within thought is, strictly speaking, the jurisdiction over thought itself of the mathematical rupture, of the intelligible power of the matheme.

Ultimately, the founding opposition is indeed the following one: Philosophy cannot begin, and cannot seize the Real of politics, unless it substitutes the authority of the matheme for that of the poem.

The deeper motive behind this opposition of the matheme and the poem is twofold.

First, and this is the more obvious of the two, the poem remains enslaved to the image, to the immediate singularity of experience. The matheme begins instead from the pure idea and afterward depends on deduction alone. This means that the poem entertains an impure link with sensible experience, a link that exposes language to the limits of sensation. From this point of view, the existence of a thinking of the poem is always doubtful, as is the affirmation that the poem thinks.

But what is a doubtful thought for Plato, a thought that would be indiscernible from nonthought? It is sophistry. It might be the case that the poem is really the chief accomplice of sophistry.

That is indeed what the *Protagoras* suggests. In this dialogue, Protagoras hides behind the authority of the poet Simonides, declaring that "the most important part of a man's education is to become an authority on poetry."[4]

We could therefore argue that what poetry is to the sophist, mathematics is to the philosopher. In those disciplines that condition philosophy, the opposition between the matheme and the poem would support philosophy's incessant effort to be disjoined from its discursive double, from what resembles it and, through this resemblance, corrupts its act of thought: Sophistry, to wit. The poem, like the sophist, would thereby amount to a nonthought that presents itself via the linguistic power of a possible thought. To interrupt this power would then be the business of the matheme.

On the other hand, and more profoundly, even presuming the existence of a thinking of the poem, or that the poem is itself a form of thought, this thought is inseparable from the sensible. It is a thought *that cannot be discerned or separated as a thought.* We could say that the poem is an unthinkable thought. Mathematics is instead a thought that is immediately written as thought, a thought that exists precisely only inasmuch as it is thinkable.

We could therefore equally assert that for philosophy, poetry is a thought that is not a thought, a thought that is not even thinkable. But the sole stakes of philosophy are precisely to think thought, to identify thought as the thinking of thought itself. This entails that philosophy must exclude from its field every immediate form of thought, something it can only do by relying on the discursive mediations of the matheme.

"Let no one who is not a geometer enter here": Plato brings mathematics in through the main door, as the *explicit* procedure of thought or as the thought that can be exposed only *as* thought. From now on, poetry must leave through the servant's entrance. This is the poetry that was still omnipresent in the declaration of Parmenides, as well as in the sentences of Heraclitus, but that obliterates the philosophical function, since in it thinking grants itself the right to the inexplicit—to what draws its power from language, rather than from the thought that exposes itself as such.

Nevertheless, this opposition in language between the transparency of the matheme and the metaphorical obscurity of the poem poses some formidable problems for us moderns.

It was already difficult for Plato himself to maintain entirely the maxim that endorses the matheme and banishes the poem. He could not do this because he had himself explored the limits of *dianoia,* of discursive thought. When it is a question of the supreme principle, of the One or the Good, Plato must admit that we are here "epekeina tes ousias," "beyond substance," and consequently that we are beyond everything that exposes itself in the incision of the Idea. Plato must avow that the donation in thought of this supreme principle—which is the donation in thought of a Being beyond beings—does not let itself be traversed by any kind of *dianoia.* Plato must himself resort to images, like that of the sun; to metaphors, like those of "prestige" or "power"; to myths, like the myth of Er the Pamphylian returning to the kingdom of the dead. In short, when what is at stake is the opening of thought to the principle of the thinkable, when thought must be absorbed in the grasp of what establishes it *as* thought, we witness Plato himself submitting language to the power of poetic speech.

But we moderns endure the linguistic interval between the poem and the matheme in a wholly different fashion than the Greeks.

First of all, because we have taken the full measure, not just of everything that the poem owes to Number, but of the poem's genuinely intelligible vocation.

Mallarmé is exemplary in this regard: The poetic stakes of the dice throw are indeed to be found in the emergence, as "stellar source," of what he calls "the unique number that cannot be another."[5] The poem belongs to the ideal regime of necessity. It subordinates sensible desire to the aleatory advent of the Idea. The poem is a *duty* of thought.

> Glory of long desire, Ideas
> Everything in me ennobled to see
> The family of irises
> Rising up to this new duty.[6]

What's more, the modern poem identifies itself as a form of thought. It is not just the effective existence of a thought offered up in the flesh of language, it is the set of operations whereby this thought comes to think itself. The great poetic figures, whether in Mallarmé—the Constellation, the Tomb, or the Swan—or in Rimbaud—the Christ, the Worker, or the Infernal Groom—are not blind metaphors. They organize a consistent *dispositif* in which the role of the poem is to engineer the sensory presentation of a regime of thought: subtraction and isolation for Mallarmé, presence and interruption for Rimbaud.[7]

In a symmetrical manner, we moderns know that mathematics, which thinks the configurations of multiple-being directly, is traversed by a principle of errancy and excess that it itself cannot measure. The great theorems of Cantor, Gödel, and Cohen mark the aporias of the matheme in the twentieth century. The discord between the set-theoretical axiomatic, on the one hand, and categorial description, on the other, establishes mathematics under the constraint of intellectual options the choice of which no purely mathematical prescription can command.

At the same time that the poem attains the poetic thinking of the thought that it itself is, the matheme organizes itself around a vanishing point in which its Real is confronted by the impasse of any straightforward resumption of formalization.

By all appearances, modernity makes the poem ideal and the matheme sophistical. It thereby overturns the Platonic judgment more surely than Nietzsche had ever desired to by way of his "transvaluation of all values."

This move results in a crucial displacement of philosophy's relation to the poem.

From this moment onward, this relationship can no longer rely on the opposition between the sensible and the intelligible, the beautiful and the good, or the image and the Idea. The modern poem is certainly not the sensible form of the Idea. It is the sensible, rather, that presents itself within the poem as the subsisting and powerless nostalgia of the poetic idea.

In Mallarmé's *L'Après-midi d'un faune* (*The Afternoon of a Faun*), the "protagonist" of the monologue asks himself if there exists within nature, within the sensible landscape, a possible trace of his sensual dream. Does the water not bear testimony to the coldness of one of the women he desired? Does the wind not recall the voluptuous sighs of another? If this hypothesis must be put aside, it is because the wind and the water are nothing when compared with the power that art possesses to stir up the idea of water, the idea of wind:

> the cool morning . . . if it resists,
> Murmurs no water that my flute does not pour
> On the grove sprinkled with harmonies, and the only wind
> Prompt to exhale from the twin pipes before
> It disperses the sound in an arid rain
> Is, on the horizon unstirred by a wrinkle,
> The visible and serene artificial breath
> Of inspiration regaining the sky.[8]

Through the visibility of artifice, which is also the thinking of poetic thought, the poem surpasses in power what the sensible is capable of itself. The modern poem is the opposite of a mimesis. In its operation, it exhibits an Idea of which both the object and objectivity represent nothing but pale copies.

This means that philosophy cannot grasp the couple that is the poem and the matheme through the simple opposition between the delectable image and the pure idea. Where, then, within language, does it place the disjunction between these two regimes of thought? I would say that it is at the point at which both of these forms of thought find their own unnamable.

In a stance transversal to the Platonic expulsion of the poets, let us affirm the following equation: Examined from the vantage point of philosophy, both the poem and the matheme are inscribed within the general form of a truth procedure.

Mathematics makes truth out of the pure multiple, conceived as the primordial inconsistency of being qua being.

Poetry makes truth out of the multiple, conceived as a presence that has come to the limits of language. Put otherwise, poetry is the song of language qua capacity to make the pure notion of the "there is" present in the very effacement of its empirical objectivity.[9]

When Rimbaud poetically announces that eternity is "the sea gone / with the sun," [10] or when Mallarmé summarizes every dialectical transposition of sensation into the Idea by the three words "night, despair, and gems," [11] or "solitude, reef, star,"[12] both poets dissolve the referent that adheres to these terms in the crucible of naming so as to give timeless existence to the temporal disappearance of the sensible.

In this sense, it is always true to say that a poem is what Rimbaud, in *A Season in Hell,* calls an "alchimie du verbe," an "alchemy of the word." But this alchemy, unlike the other kind, is a thought—a thought of what there is, inasmuch as the "there," from this moment onward, is beholden to the powers of evacuation and incitement that belong to language.

The emblem of the unpresented and insensible multiple out of which mathematics makes truth is the void, the empty set.

The emblem of the closed or open multiple, which is held at the edge of its disappearance and whose truth lies in poetry, is the Earth, this universal and affirmative Earth of which Mallarmé declares:

> Yes, I know that the Earth, far off from this night,
> Casts the radiant mystery of unprecedented light.[13]

Every truth, whether bound to calculation or extracted from the song of natural language, is above all *a power.* Truth has power over its own infinite becoming. It can provide a fragmented anticipation of a universe without completion. It can force an inference about what the universe would be if the total effects of a truth still underway were limitlessly allowed to unfold within it.

This is how, when confronted with a new and potent theorem, consequences that can redirect thought and oblige it to undertake entirely new exercises undergo assessment.

But it is also how new methods of poetic thought are drawn from a founding poetics—a new survey of the resources of language, and not merely the delight taken in a flash of presence.

It is not for nothing that Rimbaud exclaims: "Method, we affirm you!"[14] or declares that he is "in a hurry to find the place and the formula."[15] Or, for that matter, that Mallarmé endeavors to ground the poem as a science:

> For I inaugurate through science
> The hymn of all hearts spiritual
> In the labor of my patience,
> Atlas, herbal, and ritual.[16]

Though when conceived as the thought of presence upon a background of disappearance poetry is an immediate action, like every local figure of a truth, it is also a program of thought, a powerful anticipation, a forcing of language enacted by the advent of an "other" language that is at once immanent and created.

But at the same time as it is a power, every truth is also a powerlessness. For what truth has jurisdiction over cannot be a totality.

That truth and totality are incompatible is without doubt the decisive—or post-Hegelian—teaching of modernity.

Jacques Lacan expressed it in a famous aphorism from his *Seminar XXIII*: Truth cannot be said "whole." It can only be half-said [*mi-dite*]. But Mallarmé himself had already criticized the Parnassians, whom he said "take the thing whole and show it." Whereby, he added, "they miss the mystery."

Whatever a truth may be a truth *of*, one cannot claim that it affects this thing "entirely" or that it provides its integral exposition. The poem's revelatory power turns around an enigma, so that marking out the very *point* of this enigma is the powerless Real of the power of the true. In this sense, "mystery in letters" is a genuine imperative. When Mallarmé argues that "there must always be enigma in poetry," he inaugurates an ethic of mystery founded on the respect, by the power of a truth, of its own point of powerlessness.[17]

The mystery is, strictly speaking, that every poetic truth leaves at its own center what it does not have the power to bring into presence.

In a more general sense, a truth always encounters—in a point of what it has invested—the limit that proves that it is *this* singular truth, and not the self-consciousness of the Whole.

That every truth, though it may proceed to infinity, is equally always a singular procedure is attested in the Real by at least one point of powerlessness, or, as Mallarmé says, "a rock, false manor immediately evaporated in mist that imposed a limit on infinity."[18]

A truth comes up against the rock of its own singularity, and it is only there that it is stated, in powerlessness, that a truth *exists*.

Let us call this obstacle the *unnamable*. The unnamable is that thing whose naming cannot be forced by a truth. That thing whose entrance into truth [*mise en vérité*] truth itself cannot anticipate.

Every regime of truth is grounded in the Real by its own unnamable.

If we now return to the Platonic opposition between the poem and the matheme, we can ask the following question: What differentiates "in the Real"—that is, in what concerns their respective unnamables—mathematical truths from poetic truths?

Mathematical language is characterized by deductive fidelity. By this we are to understand the capacity to link up statements in such a way that their sequence is constrained, such that the set of statements obtained through this procedure triumphantly survives the test of *consistency*. The effect of constraint derives from the logical coding that underlies mathematical ontology. The effect of consistency is central. What, in effect, is a consistent theory? It is a theory such that there are statements that are impossible within it. A theory is consistent if there exists at least one "correct" statement in its language that is not inscribable within it or that the theory does not admit as veridical.

From this point of view, consistency attests to the theory *as a singular thought*. Were any statement whatever to be admissible in the theory, there would be no difference between a "grammatically correct statement" and a "theoretically veridical statement." Theory would be nothing but grammar and would think nothing.

The principle of consistency is what assigns mathematics to an ontological situation of thought [*une situation d'être de la pensée*]. It is what makes it so that mathematics is not a mere set of rules.

But we know, after Gödel, that consistency *is precisely the unnamable point of mathematics*. It is not possible for a mathematical theory to establish the statement of its own consistency as veridical.

If we now turn to poetry, we can see that what characterizes its effect is its capacity to manifest the powers of language itself. Every poem brings a power into language, the power of eternally fastening the disappearance of what presents itself. Or, through the poetic retention of its disappearance, the power of producing presence itself as Idea.

Nevertheless, this power of language is precisely what the poem cannot name. It effectuates this power by drawing upon the latent song of language, upon its infinite resource, upon the novelty of its assemblage. But poetry cannot fasten this infinite, precisely because it is to the infinite of language that the poem addresses itself in order to direct the power of language toward the retention of a disappearance.

We can therefore say that language, as an infinite power devoted to presence, is precisely the unnamable of poetry.

The infinite of language is the powerlessness immanent to the poem's effect of power.

Mallarmé represents this point of powerlessness or of the unnamable in at least two ways.

First of all, in the way that the effect of the poem presumes a guarantee that it can neither constitute nor poetically validate. This guarantee is that of language understood as order or syntax: "What linchpin do I hear, amid these contrasts, for intelligibility? There must be a guarantee—Syntax."[19] Within the poem, syntax is the latent power in which the contrast between presence and disappearance (being as nothingness) can present itself to the intelligible. But syntax cannot be poeticized, however far I may push its distortion. It operates without presenting itself.

Mallarmé then clearly indicates that there could never be a poem of the poem, a metapoem. This is the entire sense of the famous "ptyx," this name that names nothing, the "banned bibelot of sonorous inanity." Doubtless the ptyx would be the name of what the poem is capable of: to bring forth from language a coming to presence that was previously impossible. Save that this name is precisely not a name—it is a name that does not name. So that the poet (the Master of language) takes this fake name with him into the grave:

> (For the Master has gone to draw tears from the Styx
> With this sole object that Nothingness attains.)[20]

Inasmuch as it locally effectuates the infinite of language, the poem remains, for the poem itself, unnamable. The poem, which has no other role but that of manifesting the power of language, is powerless to name this power veridically.

This is also what Rimbaud meant when he accused his own poetic enterprise of "madness." Of course, the poem "notes the inexpressible" or "fastens vertigos." But it is madness to believe that it can both seize once again and name the profound and general source of these notations, these fastenings. As an active thought that cannot name its own power, the poem remains forever unfounded. In Rimbaud's eyes, this makes it a cousin of sophism: "I explained my magical sophistries with the hallucination of words!"[21]

Moreover, from his very first works onward, Rimbaud remarked the presence in the poem, understood subjectively, of a fundamental irresponsibility. The poem is akin to a power that traverses language involuntarily: "too bad for the wood that discovers itself a violin,"[22] or "it's not its fault if the brass wakes up a bugle."

For Rimbaud, the unnamable of poetic thinking is basically this thinking itself, considered *in its opening out*, in its coming. This is a coming that is also that of the infinite as it enters into language in the form of song or in the guise of the symphony that bewitches presence: "I watch over to the opening out of my thought: I watch it, I listen; I strike with my bow: the symphony stirs in the depths, or leaps suddenly onto the scene."[23]

We could thus say that the unnamable proper to the matheme is the consistency of language, while the one proper to poetry is the power of language.

Philosophy will in turn place itself under the double condition of the poem and the matheme, in terms both of their power of veracity and of their powerlessness, their unnamable.

Philosophy is the general theory of being and the event as tied together by truth. A truth is the work that takes place *near* the being of a vanished event of which the name alone remains.

Philosophy will recognize that, in summoning the retention of what disappears, every naming of an event or of the evental presence is in its essence poetic.

It will also recognize that every fidelity to the event, every work that takes place near its being and that is guided by a prescription that nothing can ground, must demonstrate a rigor whose paradigm is mathematical. Fidelity must submit itself to the discipline of a continuous constraint.

But from the fact that consistency is the unnamable of the matheme, philosophy will also retain the impossibility of a complete reflexive foundation, together with the notion that every system possesses a breaching point, a subtraction from the powers of the true. A point that is strictly speaking "unforceable" by the power of a truth, whatever this truth may be.

Finally, from the fact that the infinite power of language is the unnamable of the poem, philosophy will retain the conviction that, as strong as an interpretation may be, the meaning that the interpretation achieves will never ground the capacity for meaning itself. Or, in other words, that a truth can never reveal the meaning of meaning, the sense of sense.

Plato banished the poem because he suspected that poetic thought cannot be the thought of thought. For our part, we will welcome the poem because it permits us to forgo the claim that the singularity of a thought can be replaced by the thinking of this thought.

Between the consistency of the matheme and the power of the poem—these two unnamables—philosophy renounces its effort to establish the names that seal up the subtracted. In this sense—after the poem and the matheme, and under their thinking condition—philosophy is the ever lacunal thinking of the multiplicity of thoughts.

However, philosophy can be this thinking only if it abstains from *judging* the poem, and, most of all, from the wish (even if it is by way of examples borrowed from this or that poet) of imparting any political lessons based upon it. Most often—this is how Plato understood philosophy's lesson to the poem—this means the following: to demand the dissolution of the mystery of the poem, to delineate from the outset the limits of the power of language. This comes down to forcing the unnamable, to "Platonizing" against the modern poem. Even great poets can end up Platonizing in this sense. Let me give you an example.

§ 3   A French Philosopher Responds to a Polish Poet

Some years ago, when the socialist states were beginning to collapse, a poet came from the East, a true poet. Recognized by his people. Recognized by the prize that every year, under the guarantee of the North's neutrality, solemnly designates for the world who its Great Writers are.

This poet wished to give us a fraternal lesson. Who, then, was this "us," this "we"? "We" people of the West, and in particular "we" French, grasped through the linguistic tie that binds us to our most recent poets.

Czeslaw Milosz told us that after Mallarmé we, and the West with us, were trapped in a hopeless hermeticism. That we had drained the source of the poem. That philosophical abstraction was like a glaciation of the territory of poetics. And that the East, armed with its great suffering, the guardian of its own living word, could lead us back to the path of a poetry sung by an entire people.

He also told us, this great Pole, that the poetry of the West had succumbed to a closure and an opacity at whose origin there lay a subjective excess, a forgetting of the world and of the object. And that the poem needed both to conserve and to provide a knowledge devoted to the wealth without reserve of what presents itself.

Invited to let my sentiments be known, I wrote this brief triptych, which is devoted to the cardinal points of the question.

a) Hermeticism

Is Mallarmé a hermetic poet? It would be quite futile to deny the existence of an enigmatic surface of the poem. But to what does this enigma invite us, if it is not to the voluntary sharing of its operation?

This idea is crucial: The poem is neither a description nor an expression. Nor is it an affected painting of the world's extension. The poem is an operation. The poem teaches us that the world does not present itself as a collection of objects. The world is not what "objects" to thought. For the operations of the poem, the world is that thing whose presence is more essential than objectivity.

In order to think presence, the poem must arrange an oblique operation of capture. This obliquity alone can depose the façade of objects that generates the shadow play of appearances and opinions. It is because the procedure of the poem is oblique that we are obliged to enter into it, rather than be seized by it.

When Mallarmé asks that we proceed with words that are "allusive, never direct,"[1] we are dealing with an imperative of disobjectivation for the coming to be of a presence that Mallarmé names the "pure notion." As he writes: "The moment of the Notion of an object is thus the moment of the reflection of its pure present in itself, or its present purity."[2] The poem is centered on the dissolution of the object in its present purity. It is the constitution of the moment of this dissolution. What has been christened "hermeticism" is nothing but the poem's momentary being, a momentary being that is accessible only by way of an obliquity, an obliquity that is itself signaled by the enigma. The reader must enter into the enigma in order to reach the momentary point of presence. Otherwise, the poem does not operate.

In truth, it is legitimate to speak of hermeticism only when there is a secret or occult science and when in order to understand we require the keys to an interpretation. Mallarmé's poem does not ask to be interpreted, nor does it possess any keys. The poem demands that we delve into its operation. The enigma lies in this very demand.

The rule is simple: To enter into the poem—not in order to know what it means, but rather to think what happens in it. Because the poem is an operation, it is also an event. The poem takes place. The superficial enigma points to this taking place. It offers us a taking place in language.

I would gladly oppose poetry, which is the poeticization of *what* comes to pass, and the poem, which is itself the place *where* it comes to pass, or the pass of thought.[3]

Mallarmé calls this passing of thought that is immanent to the poem a "transposition."

Transposition organizes a disappearance, that of the poet: "The pure work implies the elocutionary disappearance of the poet."[4] Let us note in passing how inexact it is to say that such a poem is subjective. What Mallarmé wants is the very opposite: a radical anonymity of the subject of the poem.

What transposition produces in the midst of language is not an object of any sort, but rather an Idea. The poem is "a speechless flight [*envol tacite*] of abstractions."[5] "Flight" designates the perceivable movement of the poem; "speechless," that every subjective chatter has been eliminated; "abstraction," that, in the end, a pure notion arises, the idea of a presence. The emblem of this idea will be the Constellation, the Swan, the Rose, or the Tomb.

Finally, transposition arranges—between the elocutionary disappearance of the poet and the pure notion—the operation itself, the transposition, and the meaning, acting independently, in the garb of the enigma that beckons them. Or, as Mallarmé says: "The buried meaning moves and arranges, into a chorus, some sheets."[6]

"Hermeticism" is a poor word to designate that meaning is caught up in the movement of the poem, in its arrangement, and not in its supposed referent, that this movement operates between the eclipse of the subject and the dissolution of the object, and that what this movement produces is an Idea.

"Hermeticism," wielded as an accusation, is the slogan of a spiritual incomprehension of our times. This slogan conceals a major novelty: The poem is indifferent simultaneously to the themes of the subject and the object. The poem's true relation is established between thought, which is not of a subject, and presence, which goes beyond the object.

As for the enigma of the poem's surface, it should really serve to seduce our desire to enter into the operations of the poem. If we give up on this desire, if we are repelled by the obscure scintillation of verse, it is because we have let a different and suspect wish triumph over us—the wish, as Mallarmé writes, "to flaunt things all in the foreground, imperturbably, like street vendors, animated by the pressure of the instant."[7]

b) To Whom is the Poem Addressed?

The poem is, in an exemplary way, destined to everyone. No more and no less than mathematics. This is precisely because neither the poem nor the matheme takes persons into account, representing instead, at the two extremes of language, the purest universality.

There can be a demagogical poetry, which thinks it addresses everyone because it borrows its lineaments from the opinions of the day. There can also be a degenerate mathematics, at the service of the current opportunities provided by business and technology. But these are impoverished figures that define people—the ones addressed—in terms of how they are aligned with their circumstances. If people are defined, in an egalitarian stance, by their capacity for thought—this being the only sense that can be ascribed to the strictest equality—then the operations of the poem and the deductions of mathematics offer the paradigm of what is addressed to all.

Mallarmé calls this egalitarian "all" the "crowd," and his famous and unachieved Book has no other addressee than this crowd.

The Crowd is the condition for the presence of the present. Mallarmé rigorously indicates that his epoch is without a present for reasons that come down to the absence of an egalitarian crowd: "There is no Present, no, a present does not exist. Unless the Crowd declares itself."[8]

If—as we shall see, as we have yet to see—there is today a difference between East and West regarding the poem's resources, it should certainly not be ascribed to suffering, but to the fact that, from Leipzig to Beijing, the crowd (perhaps) declares itself. This historical declaration (or rather, these declarations) constitute a present and modify (perhaps) the conditions of the poem. In the naming of an event, the operation of the poem can register the latency of the crowd. The poem then becomes possible as a general action.

If the crowd does not declare itself, as it did not in the West during the melancholy eighties, and, equally, in the time of Mallarmé, then the poem is possible only in the form of what Mallarmé called "restricted action."

Restricted action in no way alters the fact that the poem is addressed to the egalitarian crowd. But instead of the event, its point of departure is the absence of the event. It is thus its malady or lack, and not its declared incitement at the heart of the crowd, that the poem turns into a material for the emergence of a constellation. Within an impoverished situation, the poet must select the elements with which to stage the sacrificial comedy of a moment of greatness. Restricted action demands that the poet create the theater of his most intimate defections—of his most indifferent places and his shortest joys—so as to anticipate the Idea. Or, as Mallarmé superbly says: "The writer, within the text, must nominate himself—of his ills, of these dragons he has pampered, or of a moment of happiness— the spiritual thespian."[9]

If today there is perhaps a difference between East and West, it is certainly not downstream, in relation to the addressee of the poem, which is always and everywhere by right the Crowd. It is upstream, in the conditions of the poem, which in the East is perhaps authorized to undertake general action and in the West is for the moment limited to restricted action. That is all I am prepared to concede to Milosz, supposing that his political predictions are to come true, something that is not certain.

The foregoing distinction affects the Idea less than its material. It separates out the operations of the poem less than the linguistic dimensions that these operations involve. Or, to borrow a category from Michel Deguy, it is a matter of knowing with relation to what aspect of the poem it can be said that this is like that. The area of exercise of this "like," from which the pure notion is born, is restricted in the West and possibly general in the East.

This is because every difference within the poem is established less as a difference between languages than as a difference within language, between those registers that the operations of the poem are capable of treating at a given moment in time.

c) Paul Celan

Is he from the East, this Paul Antschel, born in 1920 in Czernowitz? Is he from the West, this Paul Celan, married to Giselle de Lestrange, dying in 1970 in Paris, where he had lived since 1948? Is he from Central Europe, this poet of the German language? Or is he from elsewhere, from everywhere, this Jew?

What does this poet tell us, as the last poet of an epoch of the poem whose distant prophet is Hölderlin, which begins with Mallarmé and Rimbaud and doubtless includes within its scope Trakl, Pessoa, and Mandelstam?

First of all, Celan tells us that a direction for the thinking of our epoch cannot come from an open space, from a grasp of the Whole.

Our epoch is disoriented and devoid of a general name. The poem (and here we find the theme of restricted action again) must bend itself for a narrow passage.

But for the poem to pass through the narrowness of the time, it must mark and fracture this narrowness with something fragile and aleatory. For an Idea, a meaning ("gist"), or a presence to arise, our epoch demands the conjunction, within the operations of the poem, of the perceived narrowness of an act and of the aleatory fragility of a mark. Let us listen to Celan, in John Felstiner's translation:

> From the narrower slit
> a gist is coming too,
> it's broken
> by the deadliest of our
> upstanding liths.[10]

Celan then tells us that, as narrow and perilous as the path may be, there are two things that we know about it:

—First that, contrary to the declarations of the modern sophists, there is indeed a fixed point. Not everything is caught in the slippage of language games or the immaterial variability of occurrences. Being and truth, even if now stripped of any grasp upon the Whole, have not vanished. One will find that they are precariously rooted precisely at the point where the Whole offers up its own nothingness.

—Second, we know we are not prisoners of the world's bonds. More essentially, the very idea of a binding or relation is itself fallacious. A truth is unbound, and it is toward this unbound, toward this local point where the binding is undone, that the poem operates—in the direction of presence.

Let us listen to Celan again as he tells us of what is fixed (of what remains and endures) and about the transport toward, or playing in, the unbound:

> The cane that roots here, tomorrow
> will still be standing, wherever your
> soul plays you in un-
> boundedness.[11]

In the end, and consequent with the reign of the unbound, Celan teaches us that what a truth rests upon is not consistency, but inconsistency. It is not a question of formulating correct judgments, but rather of producing the murmur of the indiscernible.

In this production of a murmur of the indiscernible, what is decisive is the inscription, the writing, or, to borrow a category dear to Jean-Claude Milner, the letter. Only the letter does not discern, but instead effectuates.

I would add the following: There are several kinds of letter. There are, in effect, the small letters of the matheme, but there is also the "mystery in letters" of the poem; there is what a politics takes literally [*à la lettre*]; there are the letters of lovers.

The letter is addressed to all. Knowledge discerns things and orders divisions. The letter, which supports the murmur of the indiscernible, is addressed without division.

Every subject can be traversed by the letter, that is, every subject can be transliterated. This would then be my definition of an egalitarian freedom within thought: A thought is free once it is transliterated by the small letters of the matheme, by the mysterious letters of the poem, by the way in which politics takes things literally, and, finally, by the love letter.

In order to be free with regard to the mystery in letters that the poem constitutes, it is enough that the reader dispose himself or herself to the operations of the poem—literally. The reader must will his or her own transliteration.

This knot that binds together inconsistency, the indiscernible, the letter, and the will is what Celan names in the following lines:

> Creeping up close
> to lost footholds:
>
> two fingers
> snap in the abyss, in
> scribblebooks
> a world rushes up, this depends
> on you.[12]

In these lines, the poem formulates an imposing directive for thought: that the letter—universally addressed—should interrupt all consistency and any foothold, so that a truth of the world may "rustle" or "rush up."

Poetically, we can tell one another: "This depends on you." You, me—summoned to the operations of the poem, we listen to the murmur of the indiscernible.

But from whence does our recognition of the poem come? Our good fortune, Mallarmé underlines in a final word belonging neither to East nor West, is that "an age knows, automatically, that a Poet exists."[13]

We must concede that we are often late in allowing this good fortune to animate our thinking. Without doubt, Milosz was also pointing to this. All languages have seized hold of their own power, again and again, in admirable poems, and it is only too true that we French, so long assured of our imperial fate, have often taken years, or even centuries, to discover this.

To pay homage to the universality of the poem in the variety of its idioms, I will now say how I came to grasp the extraordinary importance of a Portuguese poet and, much further back in time, of an Arab one. I will also show how our thought and our philosophy are *composed* of such poets.

§ 4   A Philosophical Task: To Be
Contemporaries of Pessoa

Fernando Pessoa, having died in 1935, only came to be more widely known in France fifty years later. I, too, participated in this scandalous deferral. I regard it as a scandal because we are dealing with one of the decisive poets of the century, particularly if we try to think of him as a possible condition for philosophy.

In effect, we can formulate our question as follows: Has the philosophy of this century (that of the past decade included) been able to—has it known *how* to—put itself under the condition of Pessoa's poetic enterprise? Heidegger certainly sought to place his own speculative endeavor under the thinking constraint of Hölderlin, Rilke, or Trakl. Lacoue-Labarthe is currently engaged in a revision of this Heideggerian attempt, a revision in which Hölderlin is at stake and Paul Celan functions as a crucial operator. I myself have expressed the desire for a philosophy that would finally be the contemporary of Mallarmé's poetic operations. But Pessoa? We should note that José Gil has devoted himself, not quite to the invention of philosophemes that could welcome and support Pessoa's work, but at least to the *verification* of a hypothesis: that Pessoa's work—more particularly that of the heteronym Alvaro de Campos—is compatible with some of Deleuze's philosophical propositions. I can see only Judith Balso engaged in an evaluation of the whole of Pessoa's poetry in terms of the question of metaphysics. But she carries out this evaluation *from the side of poetry itself*, and not in a movement that would be directly internal to the remodeling of the theses of philosophy. We must therefore conclude that philosophy is not—at least not *yet*—under the condition of Pessoa. Its thought is not yet *worthy of Pessoa.*

36

Of course, one will immediately retort: Why should it be? What is this "worthiness" that we attribute to the Portuguese poet, which requires that one set philosophy the task of measuring up to his work? I will answer by way of a detour that involves the category of modernity. I will argue that the singular line of thought deployed by Pessoa is such that none of the established figures of philosophical modernity is capable of sustaining its tension.

As a temporary definition of philosophical modernity, let us take Nietzsche's slogan, later adopted by Deleuze: to overturn Platonism. Let us then say with Nietzsche that the century's entire effort is "to be cured of the sickness of Plato."

It is beyond doubt that this slogan organizes a convergence of the disparate tendencies within contemporary philosophy. Anti-Platonism is, strictly speaking, the *commonplace* of our epoch.

First of all, it plays a central role in the intellectual line of the philosophies of life (or of the power of the virtual), from Nietzsche himself to Deleuze, passing through Bergson. For these thinkers, the transcendent ideality of the concept is directed against the creative immanence of life: The eternity of the true is a mortifying fiction, separating each being from what it is otherwise capable of on the basis of its energetic differentiation.

But anti-Platonism is just as active in the opposing tendency, that of the grammatical or linguistic philosophies, this vast analytical apparatus marked by the names of Wittgenstein, Carnap, or Quine. According to this current, the Platonic assumption of an effective existence of idealities and of the need for intellectual intuition at the source of all knowledge is pure nonsense. For these philosophies, the "there is" in general comprises nothing but sensible data (the empirical dimension) and their organization by this veritable subjectless transcendental operator that is the structure of language (the logical dimension).

Moreover, we know that Heidegger—together with the entire hermeneutic current that invokes his name—sees the Platonic operation, which imposes the initial cut of the Idea upon the thinking of being, as the beginning of the forgetting of Being, as the inception of what is ultimately nihilistic within metaphysics. According to this position, the disclosure of the meaning of Being is already covered over in the Idea by the technical supremacy of beings, as it is arranged and enframed by a mathematical form of understanding.

Orthodox Marxists themselves had no respect for Plato, whom the dictionary of the Soviet Academy of the Sciences patronizingly depicted as an ideologue of slave ownership. For these Marxists, Plato was the originator of the idealist tendency in philosophy. They much preferred Aristotle, more sensitive to experience and better disposed to the pragmatic examination of political societies.

For their part, the virulent anti-Marxists of the seventies and eighties, the followers of ethical and democratic political philosophy, the *nouveaux philosophes* like Glucksmann, regarded Plato—who wishes to submit democratic anarchy to the imperative of the transcendence of the Good via the despotic interpolation of the philosopher-king—as the very prototype of the totalitarian master-thinker.

This goes to show that at whatever point and in whatever direction philosophical modernity may seek its reference points, one will always find within it the obligatory stigmata of the "overturning of Plato."

Accordingly, our question concerning Pessoa becomes the following: What happens to Platonism, in all of its different acceptations, in Pessoa's poetic work? Or, more precisely: Is the organization of poetry as a form of thought in Pessoa "modern" in the precise sense that it overturns Plato?

Let us recall that one of the fundamental singularities that defines Pessoa's poetry is that it offers the complete works not of one poet, but of four. This is the famous device of heteronymy. Under the names of Alberto Caeiro, Álvaro de Campos, Ricardo Reis, and "Pessoa-in-person," we possess four sets of poems that, though penned by the same hand, are so different, both in their dominant themes and in their linguistic engagement, that each of them constitutes a complete artistic configuration on its own.

Must we then say that poetic heteronymy is a singular inflection of anti-Platonism and that it is in this sense that it partakes in our modernity?

My response will be negative. If Pessoa represents a singular challenge for philosophy, if his modernity is still *ahead of us*, remaining in many respects unexplored, it is because *his thought-poem inaugurates a path that manages to be neither Platonic nor anti-Platonic*. Pessoa poetically defines a site for thinking that is truly *subtracted* from the unanimous slogan of the overturning of Platonism. To this day, philosophy has yet to comprehend the full extent of this gesture.

Even so, an initial examination seems to show that Pessoa is remarkably transversal to the century's anti-Platonist currents, having traversed or anticipated them all.

In the writings of the heteronym Campos, and especially in the great odes, we encounter what appears to be an unbridled vitalism. It is this dimension of Pessoa's poetry that authorizes Gil's hypothesis. The heightening of sensation seems to be the principal procedure in Campos's poetic inquiry, and the exposition of the body to its polymorphous dismemberment evokes the virtual identity of desire and intuition. Another brilliant idea of Campos is to show that the classical opposition of machinism and the *élan vital* is entirely relative. Campos is the poet of modern machinism and of the great metropolis, or of commercial, financial, and industrial activities conceived as devices of creation, as analogies of nature. Long before Deleuze, Campos thinks that there is a sort of mechanical univocity of desire whose energy the poem must capture without either sublimating or idealizing it, but also without dispersing it into a shifty equivocity. The poem must instead grasp the fluxes and breaks by reaching a sort of furor of being.

After all, isn't the choice of the poem as the linguistic vection of thought already an intrinsically anti-Platonic one?[1] Pessoa's approach installs the poem within the procedures of a distended or inverted logic. This logic does not appear to be compatible with the *sharpness* of idealist dialectics. As Roman Jakobson demonstrated in a fine article, it is in this way that the systematic employment of the oxymoron unsettles all predicative attributions. How is one to attain the Idea if, within the poem's strong coherence, almost any given term can receive almost any given predicate—and in particular the predicate that bears only a relationship of "counteragreement" with the term that it affects? Similarly, Pessoa is the inventor of a quasi-labyrinthine usage of negation distributed throughout the verse such that there is no guarantee that the negated term can ever be *fixed*. We can thus say that, in complete contrast to the strictly dialectical usage of negation in Mallarmé, there is in Pessoa a *floating negation* destined to infect the poem with a constant equivocation between affirmation and negation, or rather, that there is a very recognizable species of affirmative reticence that ultimately vouchsafes that the most explosive manifestations of the power of being come to be corroded by the more insistent renegotiations of the subject. Pessoa thereby produces a poetic subversion of the principle of noncontradiction. But equally, and especially in the poetry of "Pessoa-in-person," he challenges the principle of the excluded middle. In effect, the poem's path is diagonal. What it addresses is neither a curtain of rain nor a cathedral, neither the bare thing nor its reflection, neither the direct seeing in the light nor the opacity of a windowpane. The poem is there to create this "neither-nor" and to suggest that at its core there lies *yet something else* that every opposition of the type "yes/no" fails to capture.

How could this poet who invents a nonclassical logic, a negation in flight, a diagonal of being, and an inseparability of predicates, ever be a Platonist?

What's more, we could argue that at the same time (or nearly) as Wittgenstein (of whom he's not aware), Pessoa proposes the most radical possible form of the equation of thought with language games. What is heteronymy, then? We must never forget that the materiality of the heteronym is not of the order of the project or of the Idea. It is *delivered* [*livrée*] in the writing, in the effective diversity of the poems. As Judith Balso says, heteronymy primarily exists not in poets, but in poems. When all is said and done, what is really at stake is the production of disparate poetic games, with their own rules and their own irreducible internal coherence. It could even be argued that these rules are themselves borrowed codes, so that the heteronymic game would enjoy a kind of postmodern composition. Is Caeiro himself not the outcome of the equivocal work between verse and prose, as had already been desired by Baudelaire? Does Caeiro not write: "I make the prose of my verses"? In Campos's odes, there is a sort of fake Whitman, just as in the colonnades of the architect Bofill there is a fake assumption of antiquity. Is not this combination of irreducible games and of mimesis within trompe l'oeil the very height of anti-Platonism?

Pessoa, like Heidegger, also proposes a pre-Socratic step backward. The affinity between Caeiro and Parmenides is not in doubt. Caeiro fixes, as the duty of the poem, the restoration of an identity of being, an identity that would be prior to any subjective organization of thought. The slogan that we find in one of his poems—"do not lean on the corridor of thought"—is equivalent to a "letting be" and thus altogether comparable to the Heideggerian critique of the Cartesian theme of subjectivity. The function of tautology (a tree is a tree and nothing but a tree, etc.) is to poeticize the immediate *coming* of the Thing without the need to go through protocols, always critical or negative, of cognitive capture. This is indeed what Caeiro calls a metaphysics of nonthought, which in the end is also very close to the Parmenidean thesis according to which thought is nothing other than being itself. Which is another way of saying that Caeiro directs the whole of his poetry against the Platonic idea, understood as a mediation of knowledge.

Finally, while it is true that Pessoa is anything but a socialist or a Marxist, it is nevertheless the case that his poetry presents a powerful critique of idealization. This critique is explicit in Caeiro, who never stops deriding those who see the moon in the sky as something *other* than the moon in the sky, those "sick poets." However, we should also be sensitive in the whole of Pessoa's work to a very particular sort of poetic materialism. While he is certainly a great master of the astonishing image, on a first reading, this poet can already be recognized by the almost dry sharpness that characterizes his poetic diction. This is why he manages to integrate an exceptional dose of abstraction into his poetic charm. Constantly preoccupied that the poem not say anything other than exactly what it says, Pessoa offers us what we could call a poetry *without aura*. It is never in its resonance, in its lateral vibration, that the becoming of the thought-poem must be sought, but rather in its literal exactitude. Pessoa's poem does not seek to seduce or suggest. As complex as its arrangement may be, it is, in a manner both concise and compact, its own truth. Against Plato, Pessoa seems to tell us that writing is not a forever imperfect and obscure reminiscence of an ideal elsewhere. On the contrary, writing is *thought itself,* and nothing but. So that Caeiro's materialist pronouncement—"a thing is what is not open to interpretation"—is generalized to cover all the heteronyms: A poem is a material network of operations. A poem is what must never be interpreted.

Does this mean that Pessoa is the *complete* poet of anti-Platonism? This is not in any way the reading that I am proposing here. The apparent signs of the poet's journey through all the anti-Platonist stances of the century cannot conceal either the confrontation with Plato or the fact that Pessoa's *founding* will is far closer to Platonism than to the grammarian deconstructions upon which our epoch prides itself. Here is some of the main evidence for this orientation:

1. An almost infallible sign by which to recognize the Platonic spirit is the endorsement of the mathematical paradigm with regard to the thought of being as well as to the arcana of truth. Pessoa explicitly commits himself to the project of prescribing the poem the task of grasping the mathematics of being. Or rather, he affirms the fundamental identity of mathematical truth and of artistic beauty. As he says: "Newton's binomial is as beautiful as the Venus de Milo." When he then adds that the

problem lies in the fact that few people know of this identity, he binds the poem to the following essential Platonic *directive*: to lead ignorant thought toward the immanent certainty of an ontological reciprocity between the true and the beautiful.

Furthermore, this explains why the intellectual project at the heart of Pessoa's poetry can be stated as follows: What is a modern metaphysics? Even if this project takes on the paradoxical form—the infinitely subtle detours of which Judith Balso has explored—of a "metaphysics without metaphysics." But after all, didn't Plato himself, in his quarrel with the pre-Socratics, also desire to build a metaphysics subtracted from metaphysics, that is, from the primacy of physics, of nature?

I consider Pessoa's syntax to be the instrument of such a project. In this poet—beneath the images and the metaphors, as it were—there is a constant *syntactical machination* whose complexity prohibits the hold of sensation and natural emotion from remaining sovereign. On this point, in any case, Pessoa resembles Mallarmé: Often, the phrase must be reconstructed and reread for the Idea to traverse and transcend the apparent image. Pessoa wants to endow language—as varied, surprising, and suggestive as it may be—with a subterranean *exactitude* that I will not hesitate to declare algebraic. On this point, a comparison can be made to the alliance within Plato's dialogues between, on the one hand, a singular charm, a constant literary seduction, and, on the other, an implacable argumentative severity.

2. Even more Platonic is what could be referred to as the archetypal ontological basis of the appeal to the visible. This appeal never allows us to ignore that what is ultimately at stake in the poem is not the sensorial singularities themselves, but their type, their ontotype. This point is displayed in a grandiose fashion at the beginning of the *Ode marítima* (Maritime ode), one of Campos's (and the century's) greatest poems, when the real and present pier manifests itself as the intrinsic Great Pier. It is also omnipresent throughout the heteronyms, as well as in the prose book of the "semiheteronym" Bernardo Soares, the now widely known *Book of Disquiet*: In this text, the rain, the machine, the tree, the shadow, and the passerby are poetically transformed, through very diverse means, into the Rain, the Machine, the Tree, the Shadow, and the Passerby. Even the smile of the tobacconist, at the end of another famous poem of Campos's, "Tobacco Shop," takes place only in the direction of an eternal Smile. The power of the poem lies in never separating this direction from the pres-

ence—be it an infinitesimal one—that constitutes its origin. The Idea is not separated from the thing—it is not transcendent. But neither is it, as for Aristotle, a form that prescribes and commands a material. What the poem declares is that *things are identical to their Idea.* This is why the naming of the visible is carried out as a journey through a network comprising types of beings—a journey whose guiding thread is syntax. Just as Platonic dialectics leads one to the point where the thought of the thing and the intuition of the Idea are inseparable.

3. Heteronymy itself, construed as a *dispositif* for thinking, rather than as a subjective drama, directs the composition of an ideal place of sorts in which the correlations and disjunctions of the figures evoke the relationships among the "supreme genera" (or kinds) in Plato's *Sophist.* If, as can be easily done, we identify Caeiro with the figure of the Same, we immediately see that Campos is required as the figure of the Other. If Campos, as an agonized alterity in flight from itself, exposed to dismemberment and polymorphism, is identified with the formless, or with the "errant cause" of the *Timaeus*, it is clear why he demands Reis as the severe authority of form. If we identify "Pessoa-in-person" as the poet of equivocity, of the interval, of what is neither being nor nonbeing, we can see why he is the only one not to be a disciple of Caeiro, who instead requires from the poem the most rigorous univocity. Finally, if Caeiro, the modern pre-Socratic, assumes the reign of the finite, it is because Campos will in turn allow the energy of the poem an infinite flight. We can thus say that *heteronymy is a possible image of the intelligible place,* of this composition of thought through the alternating play of its own categories.

4. Even Pessoa's political project resembles the one set out by Plato in the *Republic.* Indeed, Pessoa writes—under the title of *Mensagem* (Message)—a collection of poems dedicated to the destiny of Portugal. In these poems, we are not confronted with a program adjusted to the circumstantial concerns of Portuguese life, nor with an examination of the general principles of political philosophy. We are dealing instead with an ideal reconstruction, based on a systematic treatment of emblems. Just as Plato wishes to set down the ideal organization and legitimacy of *a* universalizable Greek city, determinate, albeit nonexistent, Pessoa wants to give rise in his poetics to the precise idea of a Portugal at once singular (through the heraldic recapitulation of its history) and universal (through the declaration of its ideal capacity to be the name of a "fifth Empire"). And just as Plato tempers the ideal solidity of his reconstruction by indicating a

vanishing point (the corruption of the just city is inevitable, since the forgetting of its founding Number will bring about the demagogical supremacy of gymnastics over the teaching of the arts), Pessoa, by binding the becoming of his poetic national idea to the unforeseeable chance of the hidden king's return, cloaks his entire enterprise, which is otherwise architectonically sound, in fog and enigma.

Must we then conclude to a sort of Platonism in Pessoa? No more than we need to subsume him under the label of the century's anti-Platonism. Pessoa's modernity lies in casting doubt on the pertinence of the Platonism/anti-Platonism opposition: The task of the thought-poem is neither allegiance to Platonism nor its reversal.

This is what we philosophers have yet to fully understand. Hence our thought is not yet worthy of Pessoa. To be worthy of Pessoa would mean accepting the coextension of the sensible and of the Idea *but* conceding nothing to the transcendence of the One. To think that there is nothing but multiple singularities *but* not to draw from that tenet anything that would resemble empiricism.

It is to this *delay* vis-à-vis Pessoa that we owe the very strange feeling that overtakes us upon reading him, the feeling that *he is sufficient unto himself.* When we cast our gaze on a page of Pessoa, we rapidly acquire the conviction that he will always hold us captive, that it is useless to read other books, that *it is all there.*

Of course, one can at first imagine that the cause of this conviction is heteronymy. Rather than being the author of an oeuvre, Pessoa has laid out an entire literature, a literary configuration wherein all the oppositions and intellectual problems of the century come to inscribe themselves. In this respect, he has greatly surpassed the Mallarméan project of the Book. The weakness of Mallarmé's project lay in retaining the sovereignty of the One, of the author—even if this author made himself absent from the Book to the point of becoming anonymous. Mallarméan anonymity remains prisoner to the transcendence of the author. The heteronyms (Caeiro, Campos, Reis, "Pessoa-in-person," Soares) are opposed to the anonymous inasmuch as they do not stake a claim upon the One or the All, but instead originarily establish the contingency of the multiple. That is why, better than the Book, they compose a universe. For the real universe is at once multiple, contingent, and untotalizable.

Yet our mental capture at the hands of Pessoa results, even more profoundly, from the fact that philosophy has yet to exhaust his modernity. So that we find ourselves reading this poet and not being able to wrest ourselves from him, finding in his work an imperative to which we do not yet know how to submit ourselves: to follow the path that sets out, between Plato and the anti-Plato, in the interval that the poet has opened up for us, a veritable philosophy of the multiple, of the void, of the infinite. A philosophy that will affirmatively do justice to this world that the gods have forever abandoned.

§ 5 A Poetic Dialectic: Labîd ben Rabi'a and Mallarmé

I do not have much faith in comparative literature. But I believe in the universality of great poems, even when they are presented in the almost invariably disastrous approximation that translation represents. "Comparison" can serve as a sort of experimental verification of this universality.

My own comparison concerns a poem in Arabic and a poem in French. It forced itself upon me once I discovered the Arabic poem—late, much too late, for reasons to which I've already alluded. These two poems speak to me of a proximity in thought that, as it were, is simultaneously muted and animated by the immensity of the gap that separates them.

The French poem is Mallarmé's *Coup de dés*. Let us briefly recall what we are witness to in this poem: Upon an anonymous maritime surface, an old Master mockingly shakes his hand, cupped over dice, hesitating before the throw for so long that it seems as if he'll be swallowed up before the gesture will have been decided. Then, Mallarmé says:

> Nothing, of the memorable crisis wherein the event might have been accomplished in view of all null human results, will have taken place (an ordinary elevation pours out absence) but the place, some nondescript splashing below as if to disperse the empty act abruptly that otherwise by its falsehood would have founded perdition in these indeterminate latitudes where all reality dissolves.[1]

Nevertheless, on the last page of the poem, there arises in the sky a Constellation, which is like the celestial figure or cipher for what (down here) will have never been decided.

The poem in Arabic is one of the so-called pre-Islamic odes, a *mu'allaqa* attributed to Labîd ben Rabi'a. This poem too is born in the recognition of a radical collapse. From its very first verse, it proclaims: "Effaced, the encampments of days past and days to come."[2] The poem is born once the return of the storyteller to the encampment meets with nothing but the return of the desert. Here, too, the bareness of the place seems to have swallowed up all existence, whether real or symbolic, that was supposed to have once inhabited it. "Vestiges! All have fled! Empty, forsaken, the land!," the poet says. And: "Places once full, bare places, relinquished at dawn, / Useless ditches, abandoned tow."

But, through a very subtle dialectic that I will refrain from reconstructing, in which the animals of the desert play a central metaphorical role, the poem will move toward the eulogy of the lineage and the clan. It will end by eliciting the figure of the master of choice and of law, presented as the one for whom the initial void was destined.

> Always, we see the assembled clans call upon
> One of us, who cuts talk short and imposes his views,
> He vouches the right of those from the tribe,
> Sharing out, diminishing or augmenting, he is the sole master
> Of choices. Good, and urging all others to be so,
> Clement, he harvests the rarest of virtues.

In Mallarmé, there is the master's impossibility of choosing, the fact that, as the poem says: "The Master hesitates, corpse by the arm separated from the secret it withholds, rather than play as a hoary maniac the game in the name of the waves."[3] It is from this hesitation that first arises the menace that nothing has taken place but the place, followed by the stellar figure.

For Labîd ben Rabi'a, one begins from the bare place, from absence, from the desert vanishing. One then draws from this beginning the power to evoke a master whose virtue is that of the just choice, of the decision that all can accept.

These two poems are separated by thirteen centuries. For the one, the context is the bourgeois salons of imperial France, for the other, the nomadism of the high civilizations of the Arabian desert. Their languages share no ancestry, not even a distant one. The gap between them is almost devoid of concept.

And yet! Let us agree for a moment that for Mallarmé the Constellation arising unpredictably after the master's shipwreck is a symbol of what he calls the Idea or truth. Let us also agree that the existence of a just master, who, as the poet says, knows how to provide humans with security, how to confer abundance and longevity upon everyone's share, how to "build for us a lofty home"—yes, let us indeed agree that such a master is also what a people is capable of when it comes to justice and truth. We can then see that the two poems, in and by their gap without measure, both speak to us of a unique and singular question, to wit: What are the relations between the place, the master, and truth? Why must the place be the place of an absence (or the bare place, which is nothing but the taking place of the place), for one to be able to pronounce upon the precise adjustment of justice (or truth) to the destiny of the master that sustains it?

The poem of the nomad faced with the abolished encampment and the poem of the Western man of letters constructing the chimera of an eternal dice throw upon the ocean fill their immense gap as they converge on the question that haunts them both: The master of truth must traverse the defection of the place for which, or on the basis of which, there is truth. The poem must be wagered in the closest proximity possible to the absolute revenge exacted by the indifference of the universe. The master can confer a poetic chance upon a truth only at the point where (perhaps) there is nothing but the desert, nothing but the abyss. Where nothing has taken or will take place. This is tantamount to saying that the master must risk the poem exactly at the point where a resort to the poem seems to have vanished. This is what the ode of Labîd ben Rabi'a says with extraordinary precision. In this ode, the vanished encampment is indeed compared to a "writing eroded by the secret of the stone." A direct correspondence is established between the last traces of the camp and a text written upon the sand:

> Of the camp there remains a design bared by the waters,
> Like a text whose lines the pen has reawakened.

The poet even declares that the poetic call directed at this absence cannot really find its proper language:

> What good is it to call upon
> A deaf eternity, with an indistinct language?

It is therefore entirely clear that the ordeal of absence and of the bare place is at the same time that of a probable effacement of the text or the poem. Sand and rain will dissolve and delete everything.

In very similar terms, Mallarmé evokes "these latitudes of indeterminate waves in which all reality dissolves," and since it is a question of the master, the near certainty of a "shipwreck pertaining to man without vessel no matter where vain."[4]

Our double-edged question thus gains in precision: If the defection of the place is the same thing as the defection of language, what is the paradoxical experience that links this defection to the poetic couple of the master and truth?

We possess two versions, or articulations, of this question, one in the French poem, the other in the Arabic ode.

For Labîd ben Rabi'a, the desert experience of the abolished encampment, together with the impotence of language, leads to a restitution of the master—we could almost say to his invocation. It does this in two stages. First, in a nostalgic moment supported by the figure of the Woman—the sole reverie that can measure up both to absence and to the traces that the sand and the rain efface like a text.

> Your nostalgia again sees the women leaving,
> The palanquins, cotton shelters, curtains,
> Fluttering up there, the fine trimmings
> On the wooden cradle the shadows envelop.

Then, in a second moment, we witness a long reconstitution of energy, passing through the evocation of the nomad's racing beasts (camel or mare), as well as of the wild creatures they resemble (lions and wolves). It is as though the tribe's coat of arms were to be drawn up on the basis of this evoked energy.

Justice and the master will come to dwell at the heart of this coat of arms. The poetic path of thinking goes from the void to desiring nostalgia, from desire to the energy of movement, from energy to the coat of arms, and from the coat of arms to the master. In the beginning, this thinking situates within the Open the retreat of all things; but it then opens the retreat itself. This is both because things, evoked in their absence, possess an unprecedented poetic energy, and because the master comes to stamp his seal upon this liberated energy. Truth is therefore what a desire is capable of asserting, once it has inhabited and confronted the anxiety of disappearance.

Mallarmé's poem articulates the question otherwise. The empty place is haunted by the traces of a shipwreck, and the master himself has already been half swallowed up. Unlike in the ode, the master is not a witness looking upon absence. Instead, he is taken up or seized by disappearance. As I have already noted, the master hesitates to throw the dice and comes to equate gesture with nongesture. It is then that Truth arises, like an ideal dice throw inscribed in the nocturnal sky. We should doubtless say the following: It is the retreat of all things, including the Master, that comes first. For the Open to come, the retreat must be such that to act or not to act, to throw or not to throw the dice, amount to equivalent arrangements. This is nothing short of the abolition of all mastery, for, as the ode states in an exemplary manner, a master is one who is the sole master of choice. For Mallarmé, the function of the master is to make choice and non-choice equivalent. In this way, the master supports the bareness of place to the very end. And truth arises, in total anonymity, over the deserted place.

To sum up, we could draw the following provisional conclusions:

1. There is no possible truth save under the condition of a crossing of the place of truth, conceived here as a null, absented, and deserted place. Every truth is imperiled by the possibility that there may be nothing besides the indifferent place, the sand, the rain, the ocean, the abyss.

2. The subject of poetic saying is the subject of this ordeal or peril.

3. The subject can be either the witness of the abolition—the one who returns where all has disappeared—or its transitory survivor.

4. If the subject is the witness of the abolition, he will force language to come alive on the basis of the void—that is, on the basis of the impotence of language—until it arouses the intense figure of the master that he will thereby have become.

5. If the subject is the survivor of the abolition, he will endeavor to make it so that action and nonaction are undecidable, or so that, within the subject, being becomes strictly identical to nonbeing. Only then will the Idea come, anonymous.

6. Thus there appear to be two possible responses to our question concerning the link between the place, the master, and truth:

—Truth results from the fact that the place—the ordeal of absence and void—first nostalgically and then actively arouses the fiction of a master that would be capable of truth.

—Truth results from the disappearance of the master into the anonymity of the empty place. In brief, the master has sacrificed himself so that truth may be.

In the first case, the void of the place and the experience of anxiety create a conjunction of the master and truth.

In the second case, the void of the place creates a disjunction between the master and truth: The former disappears into the abyss, while the latter, having become absolutely impersonal, arises, as it were, above this disappearance.

We could say that the force of the second path, that of Mallarmé, lies precisely in separating truth from any particularity ascribable to the master. It is, to speak like a psychoanalyst, a truth without transference.

But this truth entails a twofold weakness.

—A subjective weakness, because we are dealing with a doctrine of sacrifice. All things considered, the master remains a Christian one. He must disappear so that truth may arise. But is a sacrificial master what we require?

—An ontological weakness, because ultimately there are two stages, two registers of being. There is the oceanic, abysmal, and neutral place where the master's gesture is wrecked. And then, above it, there is the sky in which the Constellation emerges, and which is, as Mallarmé's says, "on high perhaps, as far as place can fuse with the beyond."[5] In other words, Mallarmé maintains an ontological dualism, together with something akin to a Platonic transcendence of truth.

Turning to the poem of Labîd ben Rabi'a, we find its philosophical strengths and weaknesses distributed in a completely different way.

The great strength of this poem lies in rigorously maintaining a principle of immanence. The just master's power of incitement, dwelling at the heart of the coat of arms, is poetically constituted starting from the void place. It is a way of unfolding this "worn writing," this "text whose lines the pen has reawakened," which is experienced by the poet upon returning to the abandoned encampment. We will never have a second stage, another register of being. We will never possess a transcendent exteriority. As the poem says, even the master is "one of us," he does not lie beyond, he is not Mallarmé's Constellation.

Besides, this master is in no respect a sacrificial or paleo-Christian one. On the contrary, he is installed in the just measure of earthly qualities. He is goodness and clemency. Even better, he "regulates the gifts of nature." Therefore, he is attuned to this donation. Because he is immanent, the master invoked by the ode names the measured attunement of nature and law.

But the difficulty is that truth remains captive to the figure of the master and cannot be separated from it. The happiness of truth is one and the same thing as the obedience to the master. As the poem says: "Be happy with the good deeds of the sovereign master!" But can we be happy with what is shared out to us in accordance with sovereignty? In any case, truth remains linked here to a transference unto the master.

We have finally touched on the core of our problem.

Are we summoned to make a radical choice between two orientations of thought? The one, disjoining truth and mastery, would demand transcendence and sacrifice. Within this orientation, we could wish for truth without loving the master, but this wish would have to inscribe itself beyond the Earth, in a place indexed by death. The other orientation would demand of us neither sacrifice nor transcendence, but at the cost of an ineluctable conjunction between truth and mastery. In this orientation, we could love truth without leaving the Earth and without conceding anything to death. But we would have to love the master, unconditionally.

It is precisely this choice, and its impossibility, that I call modernity.

On the one hand, we have the universe of science—not in its thinking singularity, but in the power exerted by its technical and financial organization. This universe sets out an anonymous truth that is altogether separate from any personal figure of the master. Save that truth, as it is socially organized by modern capitalism, demands the sacrifice of the Earth. For the mass of consciences, this truth is entirely alien and external. Everyone is acquainted with its effects, but no one controls its source. In its capitalistic and technical organization, science is a transcendent power to which both time and space must be sacrificed.

Of course, the technical and financial organization of science is accompanied by modern democracy. But what is modern democracy? Simply the following: No one is obliged to love a master. It is not mandatory, for example, that I love Chirac or Jospin. In truth, no one loves them, everybody mocks and derides them publicly. That's democracy. But, on the other hand, I must absolutely obey the capitalistic and technical organization of science. The laws of the market and its goods, the laws of the circulation of capital, are an impersonal power that leave you no free perspective, no genuine choice. There is only one politics, or, as they say, "there is no alternative." Like Mallarmé's master, I must sacrifice all mastery of choice so that scientific truth, in its technical and capitalistic socialization, will follow its transcendent course.

On the other hand, wherever this scientific, capitalistic, and democratic modernity is rejected, there must be a master, and it will be mandatory to love him. This is what lay at the heart of the great Marxist and communist enterprise. It wanted to crush the capitalistic organization of science. It wanted scientific truth to be immanent, controlled by all, shared in popular power. It wanted truth to be entirely terrestrial and not to require the sacrifice of choices. It wanted men to choose science and its productive organization, instead of being chosen and determined by it. Communism was the idea of a collective mastery of truths. But what happened everywhere is that the figure of a master reared its head, because truth was no longer separate from mastery. In the end, to love and want truth was tantamount to loving and wanting a master. And if one failed to love the master, there was always terror to remind you of your obligation to love.

We have yet to move on. We are, if I may say so, between Mallarmé and the *mu'allaqa*. On the one hand, democracy, which rids us of the love of the master, but subjects us to the sole transcendence of the laws of the market, thereby eliminating every mastery over our collective destiny, any reality in political choice. On the other, the desire for an immanent and willed collective destiny, for a break with the automatisms of capital. But we then have terroristic despotism, together with the obligatory love of the master.

"Modernity" means not being able to choose reasonably in what concerns the relation between mastery and truth. Is truth disjoined from the master? If so, we have democracy. But then truth is entirely obscure. It is the transcendent machination of technical and capitalistic organization. Is truth conjoined to the master? But in this case, it becomes a sort of immanent terror, an implacable erotic transference, an immobile fusion that joins subjective trembling to the state's police power. In any case, whether the master is sacrificed to an anonymous power or whether it demands we sacrifice ourselves for the love of him, it is the possibility of choice that vanishes.

I believe thought must take a step back. A step toward what Mallarmé and the pre-Islamic ode have in common, to wit: the desert, the ocean, the bare place, the void. We must recompose, for our time, a thinking of truth that would be articulated onto the void without passing through the figure of the master: Neither through the master sacrificed nor through the master invoked.

Or again: To lay the foundations for a doctrine of choice and decision that would not bear the initial form of a mastery upon choice and decision.

This point is essential. There is no authentic truth save under the condition that truth may be chosen. That, at least, is certain. Indeed, it is the reason why philosophy, ever since its inception, has linked truth and freedom. Heidegger himself proposed that the essence of truth is nothing other than freedom. This is indisputable.

But does the choice of truth inevitably take the form of a mastery?

Labîd and Mallarmé both answer "yes." In order to sustain the ordeal of the empty place and of dispossession to its conclusion, a master is needed. The master of the Arabic ode chooses a natural and distributive truth. Mallarmé's master shows that choice itself must be sacrificed, that we must experiment with the equivalence of choice and nonchoice. Only then will an impersonal truth arise. Our situation in today's democracy is exactly the same: To choose such and such a president is equivalent to not choosing him. This is because, regardless of the choice, politics will remain the same, commanded as it is by the transcendence of the capitalist organization of science, on the one hand, and the aleatory effects of the market, on the other.

But in both cases there is an initial master who makes the decision about the nature of the choice.

I believe the principal challenge faced by contemporary thought is the following: To discover a thinking of choice and of the decision that would go from the void to truth without passing through the figure of the master, that is, without either invoking or sacrificing the master.

From the Arabic ode we must retain the conviction that truth remains immanent to the place: Truth is not external, it is not a transcendent and impersonal force. But we must not invoke a master.

From the French poem, we must retain the conviction that truth is anonymous, that it arises from the void and is separated from the master. But the master must neither be made absent nor sacrificed.

The entire question can be reformulated as follows: How can truth be thought, at one and the same time, as anonymous (or impersonal) and nevertheless as immanent and terrestrial? In other words, how can one think that truth may be chosen—in the initial ordeal of the void and the bare place—without either having to become the master of this choice or entrusting the choice to a master?

My philosophy, which assumes the poem as one of its conditions, tries to answer these questions. Let me now indicate some themes whose consideration I think necessary if we are to resolve our problem.

a) *The* truth does not exist, only truths—the plural is crucial. One will therefore assume the irreducible multiplicity of truths.

b) Each truth is a process, and not a judgment or a state of affairs. This process is de jure infinite, or uncompletable.

c) One will call "subject of a truth" every finite moment within the infinite process of this truth. This means that the subject has no mastery over truth and is at the same time immanent to it.

d) Every process of truth begins with an event. An event is unpredictable and incalculable—it is a supplement of the situation. Every truth, and therefore every subject, depends upon an evental emergence. A truth and a subject of truth do not derive from what there is, but from what happens, in the strong sense of the term "happens."

e) The event reveals the void of the situation. This is because it shows that what there is now was previously devoid of truth.

It is on the basis of this void that the subject constitutes itself as a fragment of the process of a truth. It is this void that separates it from the situation or the place and inscribes it within an unprecedented trajectory. It is therefore true to say that the ordeal of the void—of the place *as* void—founds the subject of a truth, but this ordeal does not generate any kind of mastery. At the very most, we can say, in an absolutely general fashion, that a subject is the militant of a truth.

f) The choice that binds the subject to a truth is the choice of continuing to be: fidelity to the event, fidelity to the void.

The subject is what chooses to persevere in this self-distance aroused by the revelation of the void. The void that is the very being of the place.

We are thus back at our starting point. For a truth always begins by naming the void, by voicing the poem of the abandoned place. Labîd ben Rabi'a tells us to what a subject is faithful:

> Under an isolated tree, up high, on the edge
> Of the dunes that the wind scatters into dust,
> The evening turns into a cloud of hidden stars.

This is also what Mallarmé tells us:

The Abyss blanched, spread, furious, beneath an incline desperately plane on a wing, its own fallen back in advance from being unable to dress its flight.[6]

A truth begins with a poem of the void, continues through the choice of continuing, and comes to an end only in the exhaustion of its own infinity. No one is its master, but everyone can come to be inscribed within it. Everyone can say: "No, there is not what there is. There is also what has happened, of whose persistence—here and now—I am the bearer."

Persistence? The poem, forever inscribed and lying stellar upon the page, is its exemplary guardian. But are there not other arts devoting themselves to the fugacity of the event, to its allusive disappearance, to what is *unfixed* in the becoming of the true? Arts subtracted from the impasse of the master? Arts of mobility and of the "just once"? What are we to say of dance, of these mobile bodies that transport us toward the forgetting of their own weight? What are we to say of cinema, this Deleuzian unwinding of the time-image? What are we to say of theater, in which, night after night, a piece is played, always different but always the same, a piece of which one day—the actors vanished, the sets burned, the director omitted—nothing will remain? It must be said that these are different types of artistic configurations, both more familiar and more pliant than the poem. Moreover, unlike the imperial poem, these configurations *assemble*. Is philosophy as comfortable with these arts of public passage as it is in its link—whether of mortal conflict or allegiance—with the poem?

§ 6   Dance as a Metaphor for Thought

Why does dance dawn on Nietzsche as a compulsory metaphor for thought? It is because dance is what opposes itself to Nietzsche-Zarathustra's great enemy, an enemy he designates as the "Spirit of Gravity." Dance is, first and foremost, the image of a thought subtracted from every spirit of heaviness. It is important to register the *other* images of this subtraction, for they inscribe dance into a compact metaphorical network. Take the bird, for example. As Zarathustra declares: "And especially bird-like is that I am enemy to the Spirit of Gravity." [1] This provides us with a first metaphorical connection between dance and the bird. Let us say that there is a germination, or a dancing birth, of what we could call the bird within the body. More generally, there is in Nietzsche the image of flight. Zarathustra also says: "He who will one day teach men to fly will have moved all boundary-stones; all boundary-stones will themselves fly into the air to him, he will baptize the earth anew—as 'the weight-less.'" [2] It would really be a very beautiful and judicious definition of dance to say that it is a new name given to the earth. There remains the child. The child "is innocence and forgetfulness, a new beginning, a sport, a self-propelling wheel, a first motion, a sacred Yes." [3] This is the third metamorphosis, found at the beginning of *Thus Spoke Zarathustra*—after the camel, which is the opposite of dance, and the lion, too violent to be capable of naming as "light" the earth that has begun anew. It should be noted that dance, which is both bird and flight, is also everything that the infant designates. Dance is innocence, because it is a body before the body. It is forgetting, because it is a body that forgets its fetters, its weight. It is a new beginning, because the dancing gesture must always be something like the invention of its own beginning. And it is also play, of course, because dance frees the body from all social mimicry, from all gravity and conformity. A wheel that turns itself: This could provide a very elegant definition for dance. Dance is like a circle in space, but a circle that is its own principle, a circle that is not drawn from the outside, but rather draws itself. Dance is the prime mover: Every gesture and every line of dance must present itself not as a consequence, but as the very source of mobility. And finally, dance is simple affirmation, because it makes the negative body—the shameful body—radiantly absent.

Later, Nietzsche will also speak of fountains, still within the sequence of images that dissolve the spirit of heaviness. "My soul is a leaping fountain," and, of course, the dancing body is always leaping, out of the ground, out of itself.[4]

Finally, there is the air, the aerial element, summing it all up. Dance is what allows the earth to name itself "aerial." In dance, the earth is thought of as if it were endowed with a constant airing. Dance involves the breath, the respiration of the earth. This is because the central question of dance is that of the relation between verticality and attraction. Verticality and attraction enter the dancing body and allow it to manifest a paradoxical possibility: that the earth and the air may exchange their positions, the one passing into the other. It is for all of these reasons that thought finds its metaphor in dance, which recapitulates the series of the bird, the fountain, the child, and the intangible air. Of course, this series can appear very innocent, almost mawkish, like a childish tale in which nothing may be asserted or assessed any longer. But it is necessary to understand that this series is traversed by Nietzsche—by dance—in terms of its relation to a power and a rage. Dance is both one of the terms of the series and the violent traversal of the whole series. Zarathustra will say of himself that he has "dancing-mad feet."[5]

Dance lends a figure to the traversal of innocence by power. It manifests the secret virulence of what initially appeared as fountain, bird, childhood. In actual fact, what justifies the identification of dance as the metaphor for thought is Nietzsche's conviction that thought is an *intensification*. This conviction is primarily opposed to the thesis according to which thought is a principle whose mode of realization is external. For Nietzsche, thought is not effectuated anywhere else than where it is given— thought is effective *in situ*, it is what (if one may speak in this manner) is intensified upon itself, or again, it is the movement of its own intensity.

But then the image of dance is a natural one. Dance visibly transmits the Idea of thought as an immanent intensification. Or rather, we could speak here of a *certain vision* of dance. In fact, the metaphor works only if we put aside every representation of dance that depicts it as an external constraint imposed upon a supple body or as the gymnastics of a dancing body controlled from the outside. In Nietzsche, the opposition between dance and a gymnastics of this type is nothing short of absolute. After all, one could imagine that dance exposes an obedient and muscled body to our gaze, a body simultaneously capable and submitted. In other words, a regime of the body in which the body is exerted for the sake of its subjection to choreography. But for Nietzsche such a body is the opposite of the dancing body, of the body that *internally* exchanges the earth with the air.

What, in Nietzsche's eyes, is the opposite of dance? It is the German, the bad German, whom he defines as follows: "Obedience and long legs."[6] The essence of this bad Germany is the *military parade*, the aligned and hammering body, the servile and sonorous body. The body of beaten cadence. Dance instead is the aerial and broken body, the vertical body. Not at all the hammering body, but the body "on points," the body that pricks the floor just as one would puncture a cloud. Above all, it is the silent body, set against the body that prescribes the thunder of its own heavy strike, the body of the military parade. Finally, dance for Nietzsche points to a vertical thought, a thought stretching toward its proper height. This consideration is obviously linked to the theme of affirmation captured by the image of the "great Noon," the hour when the sun is at its zenith. Dance is the body devoted to its zenith. But perhaps, and even more profoundly, what Nietzsche sees in dance—both as an image of thought and as the Real of a body—is the theme of a mobility that is firmly fastened to itself, a mobility that is not inscribed within an external determination, but instead moves without detaching itself from its own center. This mobility is not imposed, it unfolds as if it were as expansion of its center.

Of course, dance corresponds to the Nietzschean idea of thought as active becoming, as active power. But this becoming is such that within it a *unique* affirmative interiority is released. Movement is neither a displacement nor a transformation, but a course that traverses and sustains the eternal uniqueness of an affirmation. Consequently, dance designates the capacity of bodily impulse not so much to be projected onto a space outside of itself, but rather to be caught up in an affirmative attraction *that restrains it.* This is perhaps Nietzsche's most important insight: Beyond the exhibition of movements or the quickness of their external designs, dance is what testifies to the force of restraint at the heart of these movements. Of course, this force of restraint will be manifested only in movement, but what counts is the potent legibility of the restraint.

In dance thus conceived, movement finds its essence *in what has not taken place*, in what has remained either ineffective or restrained within movement itself.

Besides, this would provide yet another way of negatively approaching the idea of dance. For the unrestrained impulse—the bodily entreaty that is immediately obeyed and manifested—is precisely what Nietzsche calls *vulgarity*. Nietzsche writes that all vulgarity derives from the incapacity to resist an entreaty. Or that vulgarity lies in the fact that we are constrained to act, "that we obey every impulse." Accordingly, dance is defined as the movement of a body subtracted from all vulgarity.

Dance is in no way the liberated bodily impulse, the wild energy of the body. On the contrary, it is the bodily manifestation of the *disobedience* to an impulse. Dance shows how the impulse can be rendered ineffective within movement in such a way that it would be a question of restraint, rather than obedience. We are miles away from any doctrine of dance as a primitive ecstasy or as the forgetful pulsation of the body. Dance offers a metaphor for a light and subtle thought precisely because it shows the restraint immanent to movement and thereby opposes itself to the spontaneous vulgarity of the body.

We can now adequately think what is expressed in the theme of dance as lightness. Yes, dance is opposed to the spirit of gravity. Yes, it is what gives the earth its new name ("the light one")—but, in the end, what is lightness? To say that it is the absence of weight does not get us very far. By "lightness" we must understand the capacity of a body to manifest itself as an *unconstrained* body, or as a body not constrained by itself. In other words, as a body in a state of disobedience vis-à-vis its own impulses. This disobeyed impulse opposes itself to Germany ("Obedience and long legs"), but above all it demands *a principle of slowness*. The essence of lightness lies in its capacity to manifest the secret slowness of the fast. This is indeed why dance provides the finest image of lightness. The movement of dance can certainly manifest an extreme quickness, but only to the extent that it is inhabited by its latent slowness, by the affirmative power of restraint. Nietzsche proclaims that "the will must learn to be slow and mistrustful." Dance could then be defined as the expansion of slowness and the mistrust of the thought-body. In this sense, the dancer points us in the direction of what the will is capable of learning.

It obviously follows from this observation that the essence of dance is virtual, rather than actual movement: Virtual movement as the secret slowness of actual movement. Or more precisely: Dance, in its most extreme and virtuosic quickness, exhibits this hidden slowness that makes it so that what takes place is indiscernible from its own restraint. At the summit of its art, dance would therefore demonstrate the strange equivalence not only between quickness and slowness, but also between gesture and nongesture. It would indicate that, even though movement has taken place, this taking place is indistinguishable from a virtual nonplace. Dance is composed of gestures that, haunted by their own restraint, remain in some sense undecided.

Turning to my own thought—to my doctrine—this Nietzschean exegesis suggests the following point: Dance would provide the metaphor for the fact that every genuine thought depends upon an event. An event is precisely what remains undecided between the taking place and the nonplace—in the guise of an emergence that is indiscernible from its own disappearance. The event adds itself onto what there is, but as soon as this supplement is pointed out, the "there is" reclaims its rights, laying hold of everything. Obviously, the only way of fixing an event is to give it a name, to inscribe it within the "there is" as a supernumerary name. The event "itself" is never anything besides its own disappearance. Nevertheless, an inscription may detain the event, as if at the gilded edge of loss. The name is what decides upon the having taken place. Dance would then point toward thought as event, but *before this thought has received a name*—at the extreme edge of its veritable disappearance; in its vanishing, without the shelter of the name. Dance would mimic a thought that had remained undecided, something like a native (or unfixed) thought. Yes, in dance, we would find the metaphor for the unfixed.

It would thereby become clear that the task of dance is to play time within space. An event establishes a singular time on the basis of its nominal fixation. Since it is traced, named, and inscribed, the event outlines in the situation—in the "there is"—both a before and an after. A time starts to exist. But if dance is a metaphor for the event "before" the name, it nevertheless cannot partake in this time that only the name, through its cut, can institute. Dance is subtracted from the temporal decision. In dance, there is therefore something that is prior to time, something pretemporal. It is this pretemporal element that will be *played out* in space. Dance is what suspends time within space.

In *The Soul and Dance*, Valéry, addressing himself to the dancer, tells her: "How extraordinary you are in your imminence!" Indeed, we could say that dance is the body beset by imminence. But what is imminent is precisely the time before the time that will come to be. Dance, as the spatialization of imminence would thus be the metaphor for what every thinking grounds and organizes. In other words, dance plays out the event before the event's nomination. It follows that, for dance, the place of the name is taken by silence. Dance manifests the silence before the name exactly in the same way that it constitutes the space before time.

The immediate objection obviously concerns the role of music. How can we speak of silence, when all dance seems so strongly subjected to the jurisdiction of music? Granted, there exists a conception of dance that describes it as the body beset by music and, more precisely, as the body beset by rhythm. But this conception is yet again that of "obedience and long legs," that of our heavy Germany, even if obedience recognizes music to be its master. Let us not hesitate to say that all dance that obeys music—even if this music be that of Chopin or Boulez—immediately turns it into military music at the same time as it metamorphoses into a bad Germany.

Whatever the paradoxes, we must assert the following: When it comes to dance, the only business of music is to mark silence. Music is therefore indispensable, since silence must be marked in order to manifest itself *as* silence. As the silence of what? As the silence of the name. If it is true that dance plays the naming of the event in the silence of the name, the place of this silence is indicated by music. This is quite natural: You cannot indicate the founding silence of dance except with the most extreme concentration of sound. And the most extreme concentration of sound is music. It is necessary to see that in spite of all appearances—appearances that would like the "long legs" of dance to obey the prescription of music—it is really dance that commands music, inasmuch as music marks the founding silence wherein dance presents native thought in the aleatory and vanishing economy of the name. Grasped as the metaphor for the evental dimension of all thought, dance is prior to the music on which it relies.

From these preliminaries we can draw, as so many consequences, what I will call the principles of dance. Not of dance thought on its own terms,

on the basis of its history and technique, but of dance such as it is given ✓
welcome and shelter by philosophy.

These principles are perfectly clear in the two texts that Mallarmé devoted to dance, texts as profound as they are short, which I regard as definitive.[7]

I discern six of these principles, all of which relate to the link between
dance and thought, and all of which are governed by an inexplicit comparison between dance and theater.

Here is the list:

1. The obligation of space.
2. The anonymity of the body.
3. The effaced omnipresence of the sexes.
4. The subtraction from self.
5. Nakedness.
6. The absolute gaze.

Let us discuss them in order.

If it is true that dance plays time within space, that it supposes the space
of imminence, then there is for dance an *obligation* of space. Mallarmé indicates this as follows: "Dance alone seems to me to need a real space."[8]
Dance alone, mind you. Dance is the only one among the arts that is constrained to space. In particular, this is not the case with the theater. As I
said, dance is the event before naming. Theater, on the contrary, is nothing but the consequence of playing out an act of naming. Once there is a
text, once the name has been given, the demand is that of time, not space.
Theater can consist in someone reading from behind a table. Of course,
we can provide him with a set, a décor, but all of this, for Mallarmé, remains inessential. Space is not an intrinsic obligation of theater. Dance instead integrates space into its essence. It is the only figure of thought to do
this, so that we could argue that dance symbolizes the very spacing of
thought.

What does this mean? Once again, we need to reiterate the evental origin of any instance of thought. An event is always localized in the situation, it never affects it "as a whole": There exists what I have called an
evental site.[9] Before naming establishes the time in which the event
"works" through a situation as the truth of that situation, there is the site.
And since dance is a showing of the fore-name [*l'avant-nom*], it must de-
ploy itself as the survey of a site. Of a pure site. There is in dance—the ex-

pression is Mallarmé's—"a virginity of the site." And he adds: "an un-dreamed-of virginity of the site."[10] What does "undreamed-of" mean? It means that the evental site does not know what to do with the imaginations of a décor. Décor is for the theater, not for dance. Dance is the site as such, devoid of figurative ornament. It demands space, or spacing, and nothing else. That is all for the first principle.

As for the second—the anonymity of the body—we rediscover within it the absence of any term: the fore-name. The dancing body, as it comes to the site and is spaced in imminence, is a thought-body. The dancing body is never *someone*. About these bodies, Mallarmé declares that they are "never other than an emblem, never someone."[11] An emblem is above all opposed to imitation. The dancing body does not imitate a character or a singularity. It *depicts* [*figure*] nothing. The body of the theater is instead always caught up in imitation, seized by the role. No role enrolls the dancing body, which is the emblem of pure emergence. But an emblem is also opposed to every form of expression. The dancing body does not express any kind of interiority. Entirely on the surface, as a visibly restrained intensity, it is itself interiority. Neither imitation nor expression, the dancing body is an emblem of visitation in the virginity of the site. It comes to the site precisely in order to manifest that the thought—the true thought—that hangs upon the evental disappearance is the induction of an *impersonal* subject. The impersonality of the subject of a thought (or of a truth) derives from the fact that such a subject does not preexist the event that authorizes it. There is thus no cause to grasp this subject as "someone," for the dancing body will signify, through its inaugural character, that it is like a first body. The dancing body is anonymous because it is born under our very eyes as body. Likewise, the subject of a truth is never in advance—however much it may have advanced—the "someone" that it is.

Turning now to the third principle—the effaced omnipresence of the sexes—we can extract it from the apparently contradictory declarations of Mallarmé. It is this contradiction that is given in the opposition that I am establishing between "omnipresence" and "effaced." We could say that dance universally manifests that there are two sexual positions (whose names are "man" and "woman") and that, at the same time, it abstracts or erases this duality. On the one hand, Mallarmé states that every dance is "nothing but the mysterious and sacred interpretation" of the kiss.[12] At the center of dance there is thus a conjunction of the sexes, and it is this that we must call their omnipresence. Dance is entirely composed of the conjunction and disjunction of sexed positions. All of its movements retain their intensity within paths whose crucial gravitation unites—and then separates—the positions of "man" and "woman." But, on the other hand, Mallarmé also notes that the dancer "is not a woman."[13] How is it possible that all dance is but the interpretation of the kiss—of the conjunction of the sexes and, bluntly speaking, of the sexual act—and, nevertheless, that the female dancer as such cannot be named "woman," any more than the male dancer can be named "man"? It is because dance retains only a pure form from sexuation, desire, and love: the form that organizes the triptych of the encounter, the entanglement, and the separation. In dance, these three terms are technically coded. (The codes vary considerably, but are always at work.) A choreography organizes the spatial knot of the three terms. But ultimately, the triple that comprises the encounter, the entanglement, and the separation achieves the purity of an intense restraint that separates itself from its own destination.

In actual fact, the omnipresence of the difference between the male and the female dancer, and through it the "ideal" omnipresence of sexual difference, is handled only as the *organon* of the relation between reconciliation and separation—in such a way that the couple male dancer / female dancer cannot be nominally superimposed onto the couple man/woman. At the end of the day, what is at play in the ubiquitous allusion to the sexes is the correlation between being and disappearing, between taking-place and abolition—a correlation that draws its recognizable corporeal coding from the encounter, the entanglement, and the separation.

The disjunctive energy for which sexuation provides the code is made to serve as a metaphor for the event as such, a metaphor for something whose entire being lies in disappearance. This is why the omnipresence of sexual difference effaces or abolishes itself, since it is not the representative end of dance, but rather a formal abstraction of energy whose course summons, within space, the creative force of disappearance.

For principle number four—subtraction from self—it is advisable to turn to an altogether bizarre statement by Mallarmé: "The dancer does not dance."[14] We have just seen that this female dancer is not a woman, but on top of this, she is not even a "dancer," if we understand by this someone who executes a dance. Let us compare this statement to another one: Dance—Mallarmé tells us—is "a poem set free of any scribe's apparatus."[15] This second statement is just as paradoxical as the first ("The dancer does not dance"), since the poem is by definition a trace, an inscription, especially in its Mallarméan conception. Consequently, the poem "set free of any scribe's apparatus" is precisely the poem unburdened of the poem, the poem subtracted from itself, just as the dancer, who does not dance, is dance subtracted from dance.

Dance is like a poem uninscribed, or untraced. And dance is also like a dance without dance, a dance undanced. What is stated here is the subtractive dimension of thought. Every genuine instance of thinking is subtracted from the knowledge in which it is constituted. Dance is a metaphor for thought precisely inasmuch as it indicates, by means of the body, that a thought, in the form of its eventcal surge, is subtracted from every preexistence of knowledge.

How does dance point to this subtraction? Precisely in the manner that the "true" dancer must never appear to *know* the dance she dances. Her knowledge (which is technical, immense, and painfully acquired) is traversed, as null, by the pure emergence of her gesture. "The dancer does not dance" means that what one sees is at no point the realization of a pre-existing knowledge, even though knowledge is, through and through, its matter or support. The dancer is the miraculous forgetting of her own knowledge of dance. She does not execute the dance, but *is* this restrained intensity that manifests the gesture's indecision. In truth, the dancer abolishes every known dance because she disposes of her body as if it were *invented*. So that the spectacle of dance is the body subtracted from every knowledge of a body, the body as *disclosure* [*éclosion*].

Of such a body, one will necessarily say—this is the fifth principle—that it is naked. Obviously, it matters little if it is empirically so. The body of dance is essentially naked. Just as dance is a visitation of the pure site and therefore has no use for a décor (whether there is one or not), likewise, the dancing body, which is a thought-body in the guise of the event, has no use for a costume (whether there is a tutu or not). This nakedness is crucial. What does Mallarmé say? He says that dance "offers you the nakedness of your concepts." Adding: "and will silently rewrite your vision."[16] "Nakedness" is therefore understood as follows: Dance, as a metaphor for thought, presents thought to us as *devoid of relation to anything other than itself*, in the nudity of its emergence. Dance is a thinking without relation, the thinking that relates nothing, that puts nothing in relation. We could also say that it is the pure conflagration of thought, because it repudiates all of thought's possible ornaments. Whence the fact

that dance is (or tends to be) the exhibition of *chaste* nakedness, the
nakedness prior to any ornament, the nakedness that does not derive from
the divestment of ornaments but is, on the contrary, as it is given before
all ornament—as the event is given "before" the name.

The sixth and last principle no longer concerns the dancer, or even
dance itself, but the spectator. What is a spectator of dance? Mallarmé answers this question in a particularly demanding manner. Just as the
dancer—who is an emblem—is never someone, so the spectator of dance
must be rigorously impersonal. The spectator of dance cannot in any way
be the singularity of the one who's watching.

Indeed, if someone watches dance, he inevitably turns into its voyeur.
This point derives from the principles of dance, from its essence (effaced
omnipresence of the sexes, nakedness, anonymity of the body, etc.). These
principles cannot become effective unless the spectator renounces everything in his gaze that may be either singular or desiring. Every other spectacle (and above all, the theater) demands that the spectator invest the
scene with his own desire. In this regard, dance is not a spectacle. It is not
a spectacle because it cannot tolerate the desiring gaze, which, once there
is dance, can only be a voyeur's gaze, a gaze in which the dancing subtrac-
tions suppress themselves. What is needed is what Mallarmé calls "an impersonal or fulgurant absolute gaze."[17] A strict constraint—is it not?—but
one that commands the essential nakedness of the dancers, both male and
female.

We have just spoken of the "impersonal." If dance is to provide a figure
for native thought, it can only do so in accordance with a universal address. Dance does not address itself to the singularity of a desire whose
time, besides, it has yet to constitute. Rather, dance is what exposes the
nakedness of concepts. The gaze of the spectator must thereby cease to
seek, upon the bodies of the dancers, the objects of its own desire—an
operation that would refer us back to an ornamental or fetishistic nakedness. To attain the nakedness of concepts demands a gaze that—relieved
of every desiring inquiry into the objects for which the "vulgar" body (as
Nietzsche would say) functions as support—reaches the innocent and primordial thought-body, the invented or disclosed body. But such a gaze belongs to no one.

"Fulgurant": The gaze of the spectator of dance must apprehend the relation of being to disappearing—it can never be satisfied with a mere spectacle. Besides, dance is always a false totality. It does not possess the closed

duration of a spectacle, but is instead the permanent showing of an event in its flight, caught in the undecided equivalence between its being and its nothingness. Only the flash of the gaze is appropriate here, and not its fulfilled attention.

"Absolute": The thought that finds its figure in dance must be considered as an eternal acquisition. Dance, precisely because it is an absolutely ephemeral art—because it disappears as soon as it takes place—harbors the strongest charge of eternity. Eternity does not consist in "remaining as one is," or in duration. Eternity is precisely what watches over disappearance. When a "fulgurant" gaze grasps a vanishing gesture, it cannot but keep it pure, outside of any empirical memory. There is no other way of safeguarding what disappears than to watch over it eternally. Keeping watch over what does not disappear means exposing it to the erosion of the watch. But dance, when seized by a genuine spectator, cannot be used up, precisely because it is nothing but the ephemeral absolute of its encounter. It is in this sense that there is an absoluteness of the gaze directed upon dance.

Now, if we examine the six principles of dance, we can establish that the real opposite of dance is theater. Of course, there is also the military parade, but that is merely a negative opposite. The theater is the *positive* opposite of dance.

We have already suggested, on a few counts, how the theater counters the six principles. We have indicated in passing that, because the text possesses the function of naming within it, there is in the theater no constraint of the pure site, and the actor is everything but an anonymous body. It would be easy to show that in the theater there is also no omnipresence of the sexes, but, quite to the contrary, that what we find is the hyperbolic role play of sexuation. That theatrical play, far from constituting a subtraction, is in excess of itself: While the dancer may not dance, the actor is obliged to act, to play out the act, as well as all five of them. There is also no nakedness in the theater. What we have instead is a mandatory costume—nakedness being itself a costume and one of the most garish at that. As for the theater spectator, the absolute and fulgurant impersonal gaze is not required of him, since what is appropriate to his role is the excitement of an intelligence that finds itself entangled in the duration of a desire.

There is thus an essential clash between dance and theater.

Nietzsche approaches this clash in the simplest of ways: through an antitheatrical aesthetics. Especially in the last Nietzsche, and in the context of his total rupture with Wagner, the veritable slogan of modern art commands that you subtract yourself from the despicable and decadent grip of the theatrical (in favor of the metaphor of dance, as a new name given to the earth).

Nietzsche calls the submission of the arts to the theatrical effect "histrionics." Once again, we encounter the enemy of all dance, vulgarity. To have done with Wagnerian histrionics is to oppose the lightness of dance to the vulgar mendacity of theater. The name "Bizet" serves to pit the ideal of a "dancing" music against Wagner's theatrical music, which is a music debased by the fact that, instead of marking the silence of dance, it persistently underlines the heaviness of the play.

As the remainder of this book should amply prove, I do not share the idea according to which theatricality is the very principle of the corruption of all the arts. This is also not Mallarmé's idea. Mallarmé states the complete opposite of this idea when he writes that the theater is a superior art. He sees very clearly that there is a contradiction between the principles of dance and those of the theater. But far from endorsing the histrionic infamy of the theater, he underlines its *artistic* supremacy without thereby forcing dance to forfeit its own conceptual purity.

How is this possible? In order to understand, we must put forward a provocative, but necessary statement: Dance is not an art. Nietzsche's error lies in the belief that there exists a common measure between dance and theater, a measure to be found in their artistic intensity. In his own way, Nietzsche continues to arrange theater and dance within a classification of the arts. Mallarmé, on the contrary, when declaring that the theater is a superior art, does not in any sense wish to affirm the superiority of theater over dance. Of course, Mallarmé does not say that dance is not an art, but we can say it in his place, once we penetrate the genuine meaning of the six principles of dance.

Dance is not an art, because it is the sign of the possibility of art as inscribed in the body.

Allow me to provide a brief explanation of this maxim. Spinoza says that we seek to know what thinking is while we don't even know what a body is capable of. I will say that dance is precisely what shows us that the body is capable of art. It provides us with the exact degree to which, at a given moment, it is capable of it. But to say that the body is capable of art does not mean making an "art of the body." Dance signals toward this artistic capacity of the body without thereby defining a singular art. To say that the body, qua body, is capable of art, is to exhibit it as a thought-body. Not as a thought caught in a body, but as a body that thinks. This is the function of dance: the thought-body showing itself under the vanishing sign of a capacity for art. The sensitivity to dance possessed by each and every one of us comes from the fact that dance answers, after its own fashion, Spinoza's question: What is a body as such capable of? It is capable of art, that is, it can be exhibited as a native thought. How are we to name the emotion that seizes us at this point—as little as we ourselves may be capable of an absolute and impersonal fulgurant gaze? I will name this emotion *an exact vertigo.*

It is a vertigo because the infinite appears in it as latent within the finitude of the visible body. If the capacity of the body, in the guise of the capacity for art, is to exhibit native thought, this capacity for art is infinite, and so is the dancing body itself. Infinite in the instant of its aerial grace. What we are dealing with here, which is truly vertiginous, is not the limited capacity of an exercise of the body, but the infinite capacity of art, of all art, as it is rooted in the event that its chance prescribes.

Nevertheless, this vertigo is exact. This is because ultimately it is the restrained precision that counts, that testifies for the infinite. It is the secret slowness, and not the manifest virtuosity. This is an extreme or millimetric precision that concerns the relation between gesture and nongesture.

It is thus that the vertigo of the infinite is given in the most enduring exactitude. It seems to me that the history of dance is governed by the perpetual renewal of the relation between vertigo and exactitude. What will remain virtual, what will be actualized, and precisely how is the restraint going to free the infinite? These are the historical problems of dance. These inventions are inventions of thought. But since dance is not an art, but only a sign of the capacity of the body *for* art, these inventions follow the entire history of truths very closely, including the history of those truths taught by the arts proper.

Why is there a history of dance, a history of the exactitude of vertigo? Because *the* truth does not exist. If *the* truth existed, there would be a definitive ecstatic dance, a mystical incantation of the event. Doubtless this is the conviction of the whirling dervish. But what there are instead are disparate truths, an aleatory multiple of events of thought. Dance appropriates this multiplicity within history. This presupposes a constant redistribution of the relationship between vertigo and exactitude. It is necessary to prove, time and time again, that *today's* body is capable of showing itself as a thought-body. However, "today" is never anything apart from the new truths. Dance will dance the native and evental theme of these truths. A new vertigo and a new exactitude.

Thus we must return to where we began. Yes, dance is indeed—each and every time—a new name that the body gives to the earth. But no new name is the last. As the bodily presentation of the fore-name of truths, dance incessantly renames the earth.

In this respect, it is effectively the reverse of theater, which has nothing to do with the earth, with its name, or even with what the body is capable of. The theater is itself a child, in part of politics and the state, in part of the circulation of desire between the sexes. The bastard son of *Polis* and *Eros*. As we will now set forth—axiomatically.

§ 7   Theses on Theater

1. To establish—as we must for every art—that theater thinks. What should we understand here by "theater"? Contrary to dance, whose sole rule is that a body be capable of exchanging the earth with the air (and for which even music is not essential), theater is an assemblage. It is the assemblage of extremely disparate components, both material and ideal, whose only existence lies in the performance, in the act of theatrical representation. These components (a text, a place, some bodies, voices, costumes, lights, a public ...) are gathered together in an event, the performance [*representation*], whose repetition, night after night, does not in any sense hinder the fact that, each and every time, the performance is evental, that is, singular. We will therefore maintain that this event—when it really is theater, the art of the theater—is an event of thought. This means that the assemblage of components directly produces ideas (while dance instead produces the idea that the body is the bearer of ideas). These ideas—and this point is crucial—are *theater-ideas*. This means they cannot be produced in any other place or by any other means. It also means that none of the components taken separately is capable of producing theater-ideas, not even the text. The idea arises in and by the performance, through the act of theatrical representation. The idea is irreducibly theatrical and does not preexist before its arrival "on stage."

2. A theater-idea is first of all a kind of illumination [*éclaircie*]. Antoine Vitez used to say that the aim of theater is to clarify our situation, to orientate us in history and life. He wrote that the theater has to render the inextricable life legible. Theater is an art of ideal simplicity obtained via a *typ-*

ical attack. This simplicity is itself caught up in the illumination of the vital entanglement. Theater is an experiment—simultaneously textual and material—in simplification. Theater separates what is mixed and confused, and this separation guides the truths of which theater is capable. However, we should be wary of believing that obtaining simplicity is itself a simple matter. In mathematics, the simplification of a problem or a demonstration is often an expression of the most condensed intellectual art. Likewise, in the theater, to separate and simplify the inextricable life demands the most varied and forbidding of artistic means. The theater-idea, as a public illumination of history and life, emerges only at the apex of art.

3. The inextricable life is essentially two things: the desire that circulates between the sexes, and the figures (whether exalted or mortifying) of social and political power. It is on this basis that there have existed, and still exist, tragedy and comedy. Tragedy is the play of Great Power and of the impasses of desire. Comedy is the play of the small powers, of the roles of power, and of the phallic circulation of desire. In brief, tragedy thinks the ordeal of desire within the state. Comedy, instead, thinks the familial ordeal. Every genre that lays claim to an intermediary position between these two either treats the family as if it were a state (Strindberg, Ibsen, Pirandello ...) or the state as if it were a family or a couple (Claudel ...). When all is said and done, theater thinks, in the space opened between life and death, the knot that binds together desire and politics. It thinks this knot in the form of an event, that is, in the form of the intrigue or the catastrophe.

4. In the text or the poem, the theater-idea is *incomplete*. This is because it is held there in a sort of eternity. But as long as it remains in its eternal form, the theater-idea is precisely *not yet* itself. The theater-idea *comes forth* only in the (brief) time of its performance, of its representation. The art of the theater is doubtless the only art that must endeavor to complete an eternity by means of the instantaneousness it lacks. The theater goes from eternity to time, not the other way around. It is therefore imperative to understand that the theatrical representation that governs the components of the theater (as far as it can, since these are extremely heterogeneous) is not an interpretation, as is commonly believed. The theatrical act is a singular *complementation* of the theater-idea. Every performance or representation is thus a possible completion of this idea. Bodies, voices,

lights . . . all of these elements serve to complete the idea (or, if the theater is lacking from itself, to make it even more incomplete than it was in the text). The ephemeral element within theater is not to be located directly in the fact that a performance begins, ends, and ultimately leaves nothing but obscure traces. Instead, it is to be sought in the following conviction: The theater is an eternal and incomplete idea caught in the instantaneous ordeal of its own completion.

5. The ordeal of temporality harbors a strong element of chance. The theater is always the complementation of an eternal idea by means of a partially governed chance. Theatrical production, or mise en scène, is often a reasoned trial of chances. This is so whether these chances effectively complete the idea or instead mask it. The art of the theater lies in a choice, at once very informed and blind (consider the working methods of the great directors), between, on the one hand, the chance-laden scenic configurations that complete the (eternal) idea by means of the instant that it lacks, and, on the other, the often very seductive configurations that nevertheless remain external to and aggravate the incompleteness of the idea. Truth must be granted to the following axiom: A theatrical representation will never abolish chance.

6. In chance, the public must be counted. The public is part of what completes the idea. Who can ignore the fact that, depending on which public one is playing to, the theatrical act does or does not deliver the theater-idea, does or does not complement it? But if the public is part of the chance that is at work in the theater, it must itself be as prey to chance as possible. We must protest against any conception of the public that would depict it as a community, a substance, or a consistent set. The public represents humanity in its very inconsistency, in its infinite variety. The more it is unified (socially, nationally, civically ...), the less useful it is for the complementation of the idea, the less it supports, in time, the eternity and universality of the idea. Only a *generic* public, a chance public, is worth anything at all.

7. Criticism is responsible for watching over the chanciness of the public. Its task is to lead the theater-idea, just as it finds it, for better or worse, toward the absent and the anonymous. Criticism summons people to come in their turn to complement the idea. Alternatively, it thinks that

this idea, having, on such and such a day, chanced upon the experience that completes it, does not deserve to be honored by the chance that a public bestows. Thereby, criticism, too, works toward the polymorphous presentation of theater-ideas. It allows one to pass (or not) from the "premiere" to these other "premieres," these other "firsts" that follow. Obviously, if criticism's address is too restricted, communal, or socially marked (because the newspaper is of the Right, or the Left, or because it interests only a certain "cultural" group, etc.) it sometimes works against the generic being of the public. We will therefore count on the multiplicity—itself prey to chance—of critics and publications. What criticism must guard against is not its own partiality, which is required, but rather fashion consciousness, the copy, the serial chitchat, the habit of "flying to the winner's rescue," as well as the tendency to serve an all too communal audience. In this respect, we must recognize that a good critic—who is at the service of the public, conceived as a figure of chance—is a capricious and unpredictable critic. Regardless of the acute suffering his writing may inflict. We will not ask the critic to be just, but rather to be a learned representative of public chance. If, being above the temptations of the market, he is rarely mistaken about the emergence of theater-ideas, he will be a great critic. However, it is useless to demand from a corporation—from this one no more than from any other—to inscribe into its charter the obligation of greatness.

8. I do not believe the main question of our time to be that of horror, suffering, destiny, or dereliction. We are saturated by these notions, and besides, their fragmentation into theater ideas is truly incessant. On all sides, we are surrounded by a choral and compassionate theater. Our question instead is that of affirmative courage, of local energy. To seize a point and hold it. Consequently, our question is less concerned with the conditions for a modern tragedy than with those of a modern comedy. Beckett—whose theater, when "completed" correctly, is truly hilarious—was well aware of this. The fact that we do not know how to revisit Aristophanes or Plautus is more disquieting than it is heartening to verify that we have once again breathed life into Aeschylus. Our time requires an invention that would join, upon the stage, the violence of desire to the roles of small local powers. An invention that would communicate, through theater ideas, everything of which a people's science is *capable*. We want a theater of capacity, not of incapacity.

9. The obstacle in the path of a contemporary comedic energy is the consensual refusal of all typification. Consensual "democracy" is horrified by every typology of the subjective categories that compose it. Just try to take a pope, a great media-friendly doctor, the bigwig of some humanitarian institution, or the head of a nurse's union, and make them squirm upon the stage, burying them in ridicule! We possess infinitely more taboos than the Greeks did. It is necessary, little by little, to break them. The duty of the theater is to recompose upon the stage a few living situations, articulated on the basis of some essential types. To offer our own time the equivalent of the slaves and domestics of ancient comedy—excluded and invisible people who, all of a sudden, by the effect of the theater-idea, embody upon the stage intelligence and force, desire and mastery.

10. In every epoch, the general difficulty that besets the theater is its relation to the state. The theater has always relied on the state. What is the modern form of this dependence? This is a matter that requires a delicate estimation. We must subtract ourselves from a polemical vision that would turn the theater into a salaried profession like all others, a grumbling sector of public opinion, a cultural civil service. But we must also subtract ourselves from a concern with the simple fact of the prince, who installs lobbies of courtesans within the theater, as the servile followers of political fluctuations. To do this, we need a general idea. More often than not, this is an idea that makes use of the divisions and ambivalences within the state (it is thus that a courtier-comedian like Molière can play the orchestra against the audience of nobles, snobs, or devotees with the complicity of the king, who has his own scores to settle vis-à-vis his feudal and clerical entourage; likewise, Vitez the Communist could be appointed to the Chaillot theater by Michel Guy because the ministerial caliber of the man of taste flattered the "modernity" of Giscard d'Estaing, etc.). It is true that an overarching idea (decentralization, popular theater, "elitism for everyone,"[1] etc.) is needed if one is to maintain the state's belief in the necessity of the production of theater-ideas. In our own time, this overarching idea is too imprecise, which explains our moroseness when it comes to reflecting upon the theater. The theater must think up its own idea. Our only guide lies in the conviction that, today more than ever, and to the extent that it thinks, the theater is not a cultural, but an artistic datum. The public does not flock to the theater to be cultivated. The public is not a darling, it is not the teacher's pet [*Il n'est pas un chou, ou un chou-*

chou]. The theater falls under the category of restricted action, and every confrontation with the ratings will prove fatal. The public comes to the theater to be *struck*. Struck by theater-ideas. It does not leave the theater cultivated, but stunned, fatigued (thought is tiring), pensive. Even in the loudest laughter, it has not encountered any satisfaction. It has encountered ideas whose existence it hitherto did not suspect.

11. Maybe this is what distinguishes the theater from cinema, whose unlucky rival it appears to be (especially because they share so much: plots, scripts, costumes, rehearsals . . . but above all, actors, those adorable brigands): In the theater, it is explicitly—almost physically—a question of the encounter of an idea, while in cinema (at least that is what I am about to argue) it is a question of the passage of the idea, perhaps even of its phantom.

§ 8   The False Movements of Cinema

A film operates through what it withdraws from the visible. The image is first cut from the visible. Movement is held up, suspended, inverted, arrested. Cutting is more essential than presence—not only through the effect of editing, but already, from the start, both by framing and by the controlled purge of the visible. It is of absolute importance that the flowers cinema displays (as in one of Visconti's sequences) be Mallarméan flowers, that they be absent from every bouquet. I have seen them, these flowers, but the precise modality of their captivity to the cut brings forth, indivisibly, both their singularity and their ideality.

However, it is not by *seeing* these flowers that the Idea is grounded in thought, but rather by *having seen* them. Here lies the entire difference between cinema and painting. Cinema is an art of the perpetual past, in the sense that it institutes the past of the pass [*la passe*]. Cinema is visitation: The idea of what I will have seen or heard lingers on to the very extent that it passes. To organize within the visible the caress proffered by the passage of the idea, this is the operation of cinema. Each and every time, the possibility of cinema is reinvented by the operations proper to a particular artist.

In cinema, movement must therefore be thought in three different ways. First, it relates the idea to the paradoxical eternity of a passage, of a visitation. There is a street in Paris called the "Passage of the Visitation"—it could be called "Cinema Street." What is at stake here is cinema as a global movement. Second, movement is what, by means of complex operations, subtracts the image from itself. It is what makes it so that, albeit inscribed, the image is unpresented. It is in movement that the effects of the cut become incarnate. Even if, and, as we can see with Straub, especially, when it is the apparent arrest of local movement that exhibits the emptying out the visible. Or like in Murnau, when the progress of a tram organizes the segmented topology of a shady suburb. We could say that what we have here are the acts of local movement. Third and finally, movement is the impure circulation that obtains within the totality that comprises the other artistic practices. Movement installs the idea within a contrasting allusion (which is itself subtractive) to arts that are wrested from their proper destination.

It is effectively impossible to think cinema outside of something like a general space in which we could grasp its connection to the other arts. Cinema is the seventh art in a very particular sense. It does not add itself to the other six while remaining on the same level as them. Rather, it implies them—cinema is the "plus-one" of the arts. It operates on the other arts, using them as its starting point, in a movement that subtracts them from themselves.

Let us ask ourselves, for example, what Wim Wenders's *False Movement* owes to Goethe's *Wilhelm Meister.* We are dealing here with a film and a novel. We must indeed agree that the film would not exist, or would not have existed, without the novel. But what is the meaning of this condition? More precisely: Under what conditions pertaining to the cinema is this novelistic conditioning of a film possible? This is a difficult, even torturous question. It is clear that two operators are called for: that there be a story, or the shadow of a story, and that there be characters, or the allusions of characters. For example, something in Wenders's film operates a cinematic echo of the character of Mignon. However, the freedom of novelistic prose lies in not having to put bodies on display, bodies whose visible infinity evades even the finest of descriptions. Here instead, the actress offers us the body, but "actress" is a word of the theater, a word of representation. Here the film is already in the process of separating the novelistic from itself by something that we could refer to as a procedure of theatrical sampling. It is evident that the filmic idea of Mignon is installed, in part, precisely through this extraction. The idea is placed between the theater and the novel, but also in a zone that is "neither the one nor the other." All of Wenders's art lies in being able to maintain this passage.

If I now ask what Visconti's *Death in Venice* owes to Thomas Mann's, I am suddenly transported in the direction of music. The temporality of the passage is dictated far less by Mann's prosodic rhythm than by the adagio of Mahler's *Fifth Symphony.* We need only recall the opening sequence.

Let us suppose that, in this instance, the idea is the link between amorous melancholy, the genius of the place, and death. Visconti arranges (or "edits") the visitation of this idea in the space within the visible that is opened up by melody. This takes place to the detriment of prose, since here nothing will be said, nothing textual. Movement subtracts the novelistic from language, keeping it on the moving edge between music and place. But music and place exchange their own values in turn, so that the music is annulled by pictorial allusions, while every pictorial stability is conversely dissolved into music. These transferences and dissolutions are the very thing that will have ultimately constituted the Real of the idea's passage.

We could call the link between these three acceptations of the word "movement" the "poetics of cinema." The entire effect of this poetics is to allow the Idea to visit the sensible. I insist on the fact that the Idea is not incarnated in the sensible. Cinema belies the classical thesis according to which art is the sensible form of the Idea. The visitation of the sensible by the Idea does not endow the latter with a body. The Idea is not separable—it exists only for cinema in its passage. The Idea itself is visitation.

Let us provide an example. It regards what happens in *False Movement* when a prominent character at long last reads his poem, a poem whose existence he had announced time and time again.

If we refer to the global movement, we will say that this reading is something like a section or a cut of the anarchic paths, the wanderings of the entire group. The poem is established as the idea of the poem by a margin effect, an effect of interruption. This is how the idea passes according to which every poem is an interruption of language, conceived as a mere tool for communication. The poem is an arrest of language upon itself. Save that in this instance, of course, language is cinematically nothing but the race, the pursuit, a kind of wild breathlessness.

If we refer instead to the local movement, we will observe that the bewilderment and visibility of the reader show that he is prey to his self-abolition in the text, to the anonymity that he becomes. Poem and poet reciprocally suppress one another. What remains is a sort of wonder at existing; a wonder at existing that is perhaps the true subject of this film.

Finally, if we turn to the impure movement of the arts, we see that the poetics of the film is really to be sought in the manner that the poetics supposed to underlie the poem is wrested from itself. What counts is precisely that an actor—himself an "impurification" of the novelistic aspect—reads a poem that is not a poem, so that the passage of an entirely other idea may be set up (or "edited"): the idea that, in spite of his bound-less desire, this character will not, will never, be able to attach himself to the others and constitute, on the basis of this attachment, a stability within his own being. As is often the case in the first Wenders—before the angels, if I may put it this way—the wonder at existing is the solipsistic el-ement, the one that, be it from a great distance, declares that a German cannot, in all tranquility, agree and link up with other Germans—for want of the (political) possibility that, today, one can speak of "being Ger-man" in an entirely transparent manner. Therefore, in the linkage of the three movements, the poetics of film is the passage of an idea that is not itself simple. At the cinema, as in Plato, genuine ideas are mixtures. Every attempt at univocity signals the defeat of the poetic. In our example, this reading of the poem allows the appearance or passage of the idea of a link among ideas: There is a (properly German) link between the being of the poem, the wonder at existing, and national uncertainty. This is the idea that visits the sequence in question. The linkage of the three movements is needed so that the mixed and complex nature of the idea may turn into what will have summoned us to thought. The three movements are: (1) the global movement, whereby the idea is never anything but its passage; (2) the local movement, whereby the idea is also other than what it is, other than its image; and (3) the impure movement, whereby the idea in-stalls itself in the moving borders between deserted artistic suppositions.

Just as poetry is an arrest upon language, an effect of the coded artifice of linguistic manipulation, so the movements woven by the poetics of cin-ema are indeed false movements.

Global movement is false because no measure is adequate for it. The technical infrastructure governs a discrete and uniform unwinding, the entire art of which lies in never keeping count. The units of cutting, like the shots or the sequences, are ultimately composed not through a time measurement, but in accordance with a principle of proximity, recall, in-sistence, or rupture. The real thinking of this principle is in a topology rather than in a movement. As though filtered by the compositional space that is present as soon as filming begins, false movement, in which the idea is given only as passage, imposes itself. We could say that there is an idea because there is a compositional space, and that there is passage be-cause this space offers or exposes itself as a global time. In *False Movement*, for instance, we can think of the sequence where the trains graze each other and grow distant as a metonymy for the entire space of composition. The movement of this sequence is the pure exposition of a site in which subjective proximity and distancing are indiscernible—this is effectively the idea of love in Wenders. The global movement is nothing but the pseudonarrative distension of this site.

The local movement is false because it is nothing but the effect that follows upon the subtraction of an image (or equally of speech) from itself. Here, too, there is no original movement, no movement in itself. What there is instead is a constrained visibility that, not being the reproduction of anything at all (let it be said in passing that cinema is the least mimetic of the arts), creates the temporal effect of a journey. On this basis, visibility may in turn be attested to "off-screen" [*hors image*], as it were, attested to by thought. I am thinking, for example, of the scene from Orson Welles's *Touch of Evil* in which the fat and crepuscular cop pays a visit to Marlene Dietrich. The local time is elicited here only because it really is Marlene Dietrich that Welles is visiting and because this idea does not at all coincide with the image, which should be that of a cop being entertained by an aging whore. The slow, almost ceremonial pace of the meeting derives from the fact that this apparent image must be traversed by thought up to the point at which, through an inversion of fictional values, we are dealing with Marlene Dietrich and Orson Welles, and not with a cop and a whore. The image is thereby wrested from itself so as to be restored to the Real of cinema. Besides, local movement is oriented here toward impure movement. The idea, that of a generation of artists coming to an end, establishes itself here at the border between film *as* film, on the one hand, and film as a configuration or art, on the other—at the border between cinema and itself or between cinema as effectiveness and cinema as a thing of the past.

Finally, the impure movement is the falsest of them all, for there really is no way of operating the movement from one art to another. The arts are closed. No painting will ever become music, no dance will ever turn into poem. All direct attempts of this sort are in vain. Nevertheless, cinema is effectively the organization of these impossible movements. Yet this is, once again, nothing but a subtraction. The allusive quotation of the other arts, which is constitutive of cinema, wrests these arts away from themselves. What remains is precisely the breached frontier where an idea will have passed, an idea whose visitation the cinema, and it alone, allows.

This is why cinema, as it exists in films, is like a knot that ties together three false movements. It is through this triplicate figure that cinema delivers the ideal impurity and admixture that seize us as pure passage.

Cinema is an impure art. Indeed, it is the "plus-one" of the arts, both parasitic and inconsistent. But its force as a contemporary art lies precisely in turning—for the duration of a passage [*passe*]—the impurity of every idea into an idea in its own right.

But does this impurity, like that of the Idea, not oblige us—if we wish simply to speak of a film—to undertake some strange detours, these same "long detours" whose necessity Plato established long ago? It is clear that film criticism is forever suspended between the chatter of empathy, on the one hand, and historical technicalities, on the other. Unless it is just a question of recounting the plot (the fatal novelistic impurity) or of singing the actors' praises (the theatrical impurity). Is it really so easy to speak about a film?

There is a first way of talking about a film that consists in saying things like "I liked it" or "It didn't grab me." This stance is indistinct, since the rule of "liking" leaves its norm hidden. With reference to what expectation is judgment passed? A crime novel can be liked or not liked. It can be good or bad. These questions do not turn that crime novel into a masterpiece of the art of literature. They simply designate the quality or tonality of the short time spent in its company. Afterward, we are overtaken by an indifferent loss of memory. Let us call this first phase of speech "the indistinct judgment." It concerns the indispensable exchange of opinions, which, like talk of the weather, is most often about what life promises or withdraws by way of pleasant or precarious moments.

There is a second way of talking about a film, which is precisely to defend it against the indistinct judgment. To show—which already requires the existence of some arguments—that the film in question cannot simply be placed in the space between pleasure and forgetting. It is not just that it's a good film—good in its genre—but that some Idea can be fixed, or at least foreseen, in its regard. One of the superficial signs of this change of register is that the author of the film is mentioned, as an author. On the contrary, indistinct judgment gives priority to mentions of the actors, of the effects, of a striking scene, or of the narrated plot. The second species of judgment aims to designate a singularity whose emblem is the author. This singularity is what resists the indistinct judgment. It tries to separate itself from what is said of the film within the general movement of opinion. This separation is also the one that isolates a spectator, who has both perceived and named the singularity, from the mass of the public. Let us call this judgment "the diacritical judgment." It argues for the consideration of film as style. Style is what stands opposed to the indistinct. Linking the style to the author, the diacritical judgment proposes that something be salvaged from cinema, that cinema not be consigned to the forgetfulness of pleasures. That some names, some figures of the cinema, be noted in time.

The diacritical judgment is really nothing other than the fragile negation of the indistinct judgment. Experience demonstrates that it salvages the films less than the proper names of the authors, the art of cinema less than some dispersed stylistic elements. I am tempted to say that the diacritical judgment stands to authors in the same relation that the indistinct judgment stands to actors: as the index of a temporary remembrance. When all is said and done, the diacritical judgment defines a sophistical or differential form of opinion. It designates or constitutes "quality" cinema. But in the long run, the history of "quality cinema" does not trace the contours of any artistic configuration. Rather, it outlines the (consistently surprising) history of film criticism. This is because, in all epochs, it is criticism that provides the reference points for diacritical judgment. But in so doing, it remains far too indistinct. Art is infinitely rarer than even the best criticism could ever suspect. This is already obvious if we read some bygone literary critics today, say Saint-Beuve. The vision of their century offered by their undeniable sense of quality and by their diacritical vigor is artistically absurd.

In actual fact, a second forgetting envelops the effects of diacritical judgment, in a duration that is certainly different from that of the forgetting provoked by indistinct judgment, but is ultimately just as peremptory. "Quality," that authors' graveyard, designates less the art of an epoch than its artistic ideology. Ideology, which is what true art has always pierced holes in.

It is therefore necessary to imagine a third way of talking about a film, neither indistinct nor diacritical. I see it as possessing two external traits.

First of all, it is indifferent to judgment. Every defensive position has been forsaken. That the film is good, that it was liked, that it should not be commensurable to the objects of indistinct judgment, that it must be set apart . . . all of this is tacitly presumed by the very fact that we are talking about it. In no way does it represent the sought-after goal. Is this not precisely the rule that we apply to the established artistic works of the past? Are we brazen enough to think that the fact that Aeschylus's *Oresteia* or Balzac's *Human Comedy* were "well liked" is at all significant? That "frankly, they're not bad"? In these instances, indistinct judgment becomes ridiculous. But the diacritical judgment fares no better. We are certainly not obliged to bend over backward to prove that the style of Mallarmé is superior to that of Sully Prudhomme—who in his day, incidentally, passed for a writer of the highest quality. We will therefore speak of film on the basis of an unconditional commitment, of an artistic conviction, not in order to establish its status as art, but to draw out all of its consequences. We could say that we thereby pass from the normative judgment—whether indistinct ("it's good") or diacritical ("it's superior")—to an axiomatic attitude that asks what are the effects for thought of such and such a film.

Let us then speak of axiomatic judgment.

If it is true that cinema treats the Idea in the guise of a visitation or a passage and that it does so in the element of an incurable impurity, to speak about a film axiomatically comes down to examining the consequences of the proper mode in which an Idea is treated thus by *this* particular film. Formal considerations—of cutting, shot, global or local movement, color, corporeal agents, sound, and so on—must be referred to only inasmuch as they contribute to the "touch" of the Idea and to the capture of its native impurity.

As an example, take the succession of shots in Murnau's *Nosferatu* that mark the approach to the site of the prince of the undead. Overexposure of the meadows, panicking horses, thunderous cuts, together unfold the Idea of a touch of imminence, of an anticipated visitation of the day by the night, of a no man's land between life and death. But there is also something mixed and impure in this visitation, something too manifestly poetic, a suspense that carries vision off toward waiting and disquiet, instead of allowing us to see the visitation in its definitive contours. Our thinking is not contemplative here, it is itself transported, traveling in the company of the Idea, rather than being able to take possession of it. The consequence that we draw from this is precisely that it is possible to think the thought-poem that traverses an Idea—less as a cut than as an apprehension through loss.

Speaking of a film will often mean showing how it summons us to such and such an Idea through the force of its loss, as opposed to painting, for example, which is *par excellence* the art of the Idea as meticulously and integrally given.

This contrast brings me to what I regard as the main difficulty facing any axiomatic discussion of a film. This difficulty is that of speaking about it qua *film*. When the film really does organize the visitation of an Idea—which is what we presuppose when we talk about it—it is always in a subtractive (or defective) relation to one or several among the other arts. To maintain the movement of defection, rather than the plenitude of its support, is the most delicate matter. Especially when the formalist path, which leads to supposedly "pure" filmic operations, presents us with an impasse. Let us repeat: In cinema, nothing is pure. Cinema is internally and integrally contaminated by its situation as the "plus-one" of arts.

For example, consider once again the long crossing of the canals at the beginning of Visconti's *Death in Venice*. The idea that passes here—and that the rest of the film both sutures and cancels—is that of a man who did what he had to do in his existence and who is consequently in suspense, awaiting either an end or another life. This idea is organized through the disparate convergence of a number of ingredients: There is the face of the actor Dirk Bogarde, the particular quality of opacity and interrogation carried by this face, a factor that really does belong to the art of the actor, whether we like it or not. There are the innumerable artistic echoes of the Venetian style, all of which are in fact connected to the theme of what is finished, settled, retired from history—pictorial themes already present in Guardi or Canaletto, literary themes from Rousseau to Proust. For us, in this type of visitor to the great European palaces there are echoes of the subtle uncertainty that is woven into the heroes of Henry James, for example. Finally, in Mahler's music there is also the distended and exasperated achievement, marked by an all-encompassing melancholy, that belongs to the tonal symphony and its use of timbre (here represented by the strings alone). Moreover, one can easily show how these ingredients both amplify and corrode one another in a sort of decomposition by excess that precisely serves to present the idea as both passage and impurity. But what here is, strictly speaking, the film?

After all, cinema is nothing but takes and editing. There is nothing else. What I mean is this: There is nothing else that would constitute "the film." It is therefore necessary to argue that, viewed from the vantage point of the axiomatic judgment, a film is what exposes the passage of the idea in accordance with the take and the editing. How does the idea come to its take [*prise*], how is it overtaken [*sur-prise*]? And how is it edited, assembled? But, above all, the question is the following: What singularity is revealed in the fact of being taken and edited in the disparate "plus-one" of the arts that we could not previously think or know about the idea?

In the example of Visconti's film it is clear that take and editing conspire to establish a duration. An excessive duration that is homogeneous with the empty perpetuation of Venice and the stagnation of Mahler's adagio, as well as with the performance of an immobile and inactive actor of whom only the face is, interminably, required. Consequently, in terms of the idea of a man whose being (or desire) is in a state of suspension, what this captures is that on his own, such a man is indeed immobile. The ancient resources have dried up. The new possibilities are absent. The filmic duration—composed from an assortment of several arts consigned to their shortcomings—is the visitation of a subjective immobility. This is what a man is when he is given over to the whim of an encounter. A man, as Samuel Beckett would say, "immobile in the dark," until the incalculable delight of his torturer, of his new desire, comes upon him—if indeed it does come.

Now, the fact that it is the immobile side of the idea that is brought forward here is precisely what makes for a passage. One could show that the other arts either deliver their idea as a donation (at the summit of these arts stands painting) or invent a pure time of the Idea, exploring the configurations that the influence of thinking may adopt (at the summit of these arts stands music). By means of the possibility that is proper to it—of amalgamating the other arts, through takes and montage, without presenting them—cinema can, and must, organize the passage of the immobile.

But cinema must also organize the immobility of passage. We could easily show this through the relation that some of Straub's shots entertain with the literary text, with its scansion and its progression. Alternatively, we could turn to the dialectic established at the beginning of Tati's *Playtime* between the movement of a crowd and the vacuity of what could be termed its atomic composition. That is how Tati treats space as a condition for the passage of the immobile. Speaking of a film axiomatically will always be potentially deceptive, since it will always be exposed to the risk of turning the film in question into nothing more than a chaotic rival of the primordial arts. But we can still hold on to the thread of our argument. The imperative remains that of demonstrating how a particular film lets us travel with a particular idea in such a way that we might discover what nothing else could lead us to discover: that, as Plato already thought, the impurity of the Idea is always tied to the passing of an immobility or to the immobility of a passage. Which is why we forget ideas.

Against forgetting, Plato invokes the myth of a first vision and a reminiscence. To speak of a film is always to speak of a reminiscence: What occurrence—what reminiscence—is a given idea capable of, capable of *for us?* This is the point treated by every true film, one idea at a time. Cinema treats the ties that bind together movement and rest, forgetting and reminiscence, the impure. Not so much what we know as what we *can* know. To speak of a film is less to speak of the resources of thought than of its possibilities—that is, once its resources, in the guise of the other arts, are guaranteed. To indicate what there could be, beyond what there is. Or again: How the "impurification" of the true clears the path for other purities.

That is how cinema inverts the literary imperative, which can be expressed as follows: To make it so that the purification of impure language clears the path for unpredictable impurities. The risks involved are also opposite ones. Cinema, this great "impurifier," always risks being liked too much and thus becoming a figure of abasement. True literature, which is a rigorous purification, risks exaggeration by a proximity to the concept in which the effect of art is exhausted and prose (or the poem) is sutured to philosophy.

Samuel Beckett, who had a great love of cinema and who also wrote-directed a film (the very Platonic title of which is *Film*—*the* Film, that is), loved to gnaw at the edges of the peril to which all high literature exposes itself: no longer to produce unheard-of impurities, but to wallow in the apparent purity of the concept. In short, to philosophize. And therefore: to register truths, rather than producing them. Of this wandering at the edges, *Worstward Ho* remains the most accomplished witness.

§ 9   Being, Existence, Thought: Prose and Concept

a) The Between-Languages and the Shorthand of Being

Samuel Beckett wrote *Worstward Ho* in 1982 and published it in 1983.[1] It is, together with *Stirrings Still*, a testamental text. Beckett did not translate it into French, so that *Worstward Ho* expresses the Real of the English language as Samuel Beckett's mother tongue. To my knowledge, all of his texts written in French were translated by Beckett himself into English.[2] There are instead some texts written in English that he did not translate into French that, for this exceptional artist of the French language, are akin to the remnants of something more originary within English.[3] Nevertheless, it is said that Samuel Beckett considered this text "untranslatable." We can therefore say that *Worstward Ho* is tied to the English language in such a singular manner that its linguistic migration proves particularly arduous.

Since in this essay we will study the French version of the text, we cannot consider it in terms of its literal poetics. The French text we are dealing with, which is altogether remarkable, is not exactly by Samuel Beckett. It belongs in part to Edith Fournier, the translator. We cannot immediately approach the signification of this text by way of its letter, for it really is a *translation*.

In Beckett's case, the problem of translation is complex, since he himself was situated at the interval of two languages. The question of knowing which text translates which is an almost undecidable one. Nevertheless, Beckett always called the passage from one language to another a "translation," even if upon closer inspection there are significant differences between the French and English "variants," differences bearing not only on the poetics of language, but on its philosophical tone. There is a kind of humorous pragmatism in the English text that is not exactly present in the French, and there is a conceptual sincerity to the French text that is softened and sometimes, in my view, just a bit watered down in the English. In *Worstward Ho*, we have an absolutely English text, with no French variant, on the one hand, and a translation in the usual sense, on the other. Hence the obligation of finding support for our argument in the meaning rather than the letter.

A second difficulty derives from the fact that this text is—in an absolutely conscious fashion—a recapitulatory text, that is, one that takes stock of the whole of Samuel Beckett's intellectual enterprise. To study it thoroughly, it would be necessary to show how it is woven out of a dense network of allusions to prior texts, as well as of returns to their theoretical hypotheses—to be reexamined, possibly contradicted or modified, and refined—and, moreover, how it functions as a sort of filter through which the multiplicity of Beckett's writings is made to pass, thereby reducing Beckett's work to its fundamental hypothetical system.

Having said this, if we compound these two difficulties, it is entirely possible to take *Worstward Ho* as a short philosophical treatise, as a treatment in shorthand of the question of being. Unlike the earlier texts, it is not governed by a sort of latent poem. It is not a text that penetrates into the singularity and power of comparison that belong to language—like *Ill Seen Ill Said*, for example. It maintains a very deliberate and abstract dryness, which is offset, especially in the English original, by an extreme attention to rhythm. We could thus say that as a text it tends to offer up the rhythm of thought, rather than its configuration, while for *Ill Seen Ill Said*, the opposite is true. This is why we can approach *Worstward Ho* conceptually without thereby betraying it. Since it allows us to put together a table of contents for the entirety of Beckett's work, it is entirely apposite to treat this text as if it were, above all, a network of thought or shorthand of the question of being. What we will lose in this operation—what I called the "rhythm"—is the figure of scansion (the linguistic segments are generally extremely brief: just a few words), that is, the stenographic figure belonging to the text, which in English is matched by a kind of pulsation within the language that is altogether unique.

b) Saying, Being, Thought

Cap au pire (an admirable French translation for the title of *Worstward Ho*) presents us with an extremely dense plot, organized—like in all the later Beckett—into paragraphs. A first reading shows us that this plot develops four central conceptual themes into their respective questions (I will explain in a moment what must be understood by "question").

The first theme is the imperative of saying. This is a very old Beckettian theme, the most recognizable, but in certain regards also the most unrecognized of his themes. The imperative of saying is the prescription of the "again," understood as the *incipit* of the written text and determining it as a continuation. In Beckett, to commence is always to "continue." Nothing commences that is not already under the prescription of the again or of *re*commencing, under the supposition of a commencement that itself never commenced. We can thus say that the text is circumscribed by the imperative of saying. It begins with:

On. Say on. Be said on. Somehow on. (89)

And ends with:

Said nohow on. (116)

Thus, we can also summarize *Worstward Ho* by the passage from "Be said on" to "Said nohow on." The text presents the possibility of the "nohow on" as a fundamental alteration of the "on." The negation ("nohow") attests to the fact that there is no more "on." But in truth, given the "be said," the "nohow on" is a variant of the "on" and remains constrained by the imperative of saying.

The second theme—the immediate and mandatory correlate of the first throughout Beckett's work—is that of pure being, of the "there is" as such. The imperative of saying is immediately correlated to that about which there is something *to* say, in other words, the "there is" itself. Besides the fact that there is the imperative of saying, there is the "there is."

The "there is," or pure being, has two names, and not just one: "the void" and "the dim." This is a problem of considerable importance. Let us note at once that with respect to these two names—void and dim—we discern, or at least appear to discern, a subordination: The void is subordinated to the dim *in the exercise of disappearance*, which constitutes the essential testing ground of *Worstward Ho*. The maxim is the following:

Void cannot go. Save dim go. Then all go. (97)

Once it is obliged to prove itself through the crucial ordeal of disappearance, the void has no autonomy. It is dependent on the disappearance of the all, which is, as such, the disappearance of the dim. If the "all go"— that is, the "there is" thought as nothingness—is named by the dim, the void is necessarily a subordinate nomination. If we accept that the "there is" is what is there in the ordeal of its own nothingness, the fact that disappearance is subordinated to the disappearance of the dim makes "dim" [*pénombre*] into the eminent name of being.

The third theme is what could be referred to as "the inscribed *in* being." This is a question of what is proposed from the standpoint of being [*du point de l'être*], or again, a question about what appears in the dim. The inscribed is what the dim as dim arranges within the order of appearance.

Insofar as "dim" is the eminent name of being, the inscribed is what appears in the dim. But one can also say that it is what is given in an interval of the void. This is because things will be pronounced upon according to the two possible names of the "there is." On the one hand, there is what appears in the dim, what the dim allows to appear as a shade—as the shade in the dim [*l'ombre dans la pénombre*]. On the other, there is what makes the void appear as an interval, in the gap of what appears, and consequently as a corruption of the void—if the void is determined as being nothing but difference or separation. This explains how Beckett could name the universe, that is, the entirety of what appears as follows: A void infested by shades. This manner that the void has of being infested by shades means that it is reduced to being the figure of an interval among the shades. But let us not forget that this interval among the shades is ultimately nothing but the dim, what returns us to the dim as the archioriginal exposition of being.

We can also say that the inscribed in being—the shades—is what allows itself to be counted. The science of number—of the number of shades— is a fundamental theme in Beckett. What is not being as such, but is instead proposed or inscribed in being, is what lets itself be counted, what pertains to plurality, what is of the order of number. Number is obviously not an attribute of the void or the dim: Void and dim do not let themselves be counted. Instead, it is the inscribed in being that lets itself be counted. And it lets itself be counted primordially: 1, 2, 3.

A last variant: The inscribed in being is what can worsen. "Worsen ing"—an essential theme in *Worstward Ho*, where worsening is one of the text's radical operations—means, among other things, but above all, to be iller said than said already [*être plus mal dit que déjà dit*].

Under this multiplicity of attributes—what is apparent in the dim, what constitutes an interval with respect to the void, what lets itself be counted, what is susceptible to worsening or to being iller said than said—there is the generic name: "the shades." We can say that the shades are what is exposed in the dim. The shades are the exposed plural of the "there is," which manifests itself here under the name of dim.

In *Worstward Ho*, the presentation of shades will be minimal: The count will go up to three. We shall see why it can go no lower. Categorially, once you count what lets itself be counted, you must at least count to three.

The first shade is the standing shade, which counts as one.[4] In truth, it is *the* one. The standing shade will also be found "kneeling"—these metamorphoses should elicit no surprise—or "bowed." These are different names. They are not so much states as names. Of this shade that counts as one, it is said—from page 108 on—that it is an old woman:

Nothing to show a woman's and yet a woman's.

And Beckett immediately adds (this will be clarified later):

Oozed from softening soft the word woman's.

These are the fundamental attributes of the one: The one is the kneeling shade and it is *a* woman.

Then there is the pair, which counts as two. The pair is the sole shade that counts as two. Beckett will say: "Two free and two as one"—one shade. And once the pair is named, it is established that the shades that constitute it are an old man and a child.

Let us remark that the one is not called woman until much later, while the two is named "old man and child" right away. What will be said later, instead, is that nothing has proven that we were indeed dealing with an old man and a child. In all these instances—with regard to the question of the determinations "man," "woman," "child"—nothing provides proof, and yet it is the case. Simply put, the modality of saying is not the same for the one-woman and for the two-man-child. Of the one it is not said until much later that it is an old woman, while the composition of the pair is immediately declared (old man–child); the crucial statement returns: Nothing proves that, and yet. This indicates that the masculine sexuated position is evident, and that the impossibility of proving it is difficult to understand. On the contrary, since the feminine sexuated position is not evident, the impossibility of proving it is.

In the pair it is obviously a question of the other, of "the-one-and-the-other."

The other is here designated by its internal duplicity, by the fact that it is two. It is a two that is the same. It is, let us say it again: "Two free [shades] and two as one." But, *a contrario*, it is the one that turns into two: the old man and the child. We must suppose that old man and child are the same man qua shade, that is to say, human life qua shade in its extreme of infancy and its extreme of old age, a life given in what splits it in two, in the unity of the pair that it is qua alterity to itself.

In the end, we can say that the inscribed in being is visible humanity: woman as one and as inclination, man as double in the unity of number. The pertinent ages are the extreme ones, as is always the case in Beckett: infant and old man. The adult is almost an ignored category, an insignificant category.

Finally, the fourth theme is thought—as is to be expected. In and by thought the configurations of visible humanity and the imperative of saying exist simultaneously.

Thought is the recollection of the first and third themes: There is the imperative of saying, there is the inscribed in being, and this is "for" and "in" thought. Let us note right away that Beckett's question is the following: Knowing that thought (the fourth theme) is the focal point or the recollection of the imperative of saying (the first theme) and of the arrangement of visible humanity—that is, of the shades (third theme)—what can thought say about the second theme, that is, about the question of being? This provides the broadest possible organization for the text as a whole. The philosophical construction of the question will go like this: What can be pronounced about the "there is" qua "there is" from the vantage point of thought, in which the imperative of saying and the modification of the shades (i.e. the circulation of visible humanity) are given simultaneously?

In the figural register of *Worstward Ho*, thought is represented by a head. One will speak of "*the* head" or "*the* skull." The head is repeatedly called the "seat and germ of all." If it is referred to in this way, it is because both the imperative of saying and the shades exist for the head, and it is in the head that the question of being takes place.

What is the composition of thought? If reduced to its absolutely primordial constituents—according to the procedure of simplification that constitutes Beckett's organic method—there is the visible and there is the imperative of saying. There is "ill seen ill said." This is thought: "ill seen ill said." It follows from this that the presentation of the head will be essentially reduced to its eyes, on the one hand, and to its brain, oozing words, on the other: Two holes on a brain, this is thought.

Hence two recurrent themes: That of the eyes and that of the oozing of words, whose source is the soft matter of the brain. This is the material figure of spirit.

Let us be more precise.

It will be said that the eyes are "clenched staring." The "movement" of staring is essential to *Worstward Ho.* It designates seeing as such. This "clenched staring"—obviously an abrupt juxtaposition—designates precisely the emblem of the ill seen. Seeing is always an ill seeing, and consequently the eye of seeing is "clenched staring."

As for words—the second attribute of thought after seeing—one will say "somehow from some soft mind they ooze." These two maxims, the existence of "clenched staring eyes" and the fact that words "somehow from some soft mind . . . ooze," determine the fourth theme, that is, thought in the modality of existence represented by the skull.

It is of capital importance to note that the skull is a supplementary shade. The skull makes three, *besides* the one of feminine inclination and the other—in the guise of the pair—of the old man and the child. Thought always comes third. On page 98, we find an essential recapitulation of these themes:

From now one for the kneeling one. As from now two for the twain. The as one plodding twain. As from now three for the head.

When Beckett counts the pair, he does indeed note that it falls under the two, but that it is not two, it is *the* two. The pair is the two, but added to the one, it does not make three. By adding the pair to the one, you still have two, the two of the other after the one. Only the head makes three. The three is thought.

c) The Indispensable Three-Thought

We must note that Beckett's text often functions by means of radical attempts that are in turn renounced by Beckett from within the text itself. It is thus that the head is adjoined—that is, it comes in third place—after a materialist attempt to do without it, an attempt where there would be nothing but the place and the body.

At the very beginning, Beckett says: a place, a body. "No mind. Where none. That at least." As if to say: "that's something, anyway." One will act as if everything happened within a space of integral materiality. But this attempt will fail. In the end, one is forced to add the head, which in Beckett's vocabulary means that there are always remains of mind. These are precisely the clenched staring eyes, on the one hand, and the *on* of the oozing of words from the soft matter of the brain, on the other.

This remainder of mind that finds its figure in the head will be the supplement required by the One and the Two of shades. Beckett deduces the ineluctable Three. But if the head counts for three, it must itself be in the dim. It is not outside the dim. One of the text's subtler turns poses that the pure materialist attempt—that is, there is nothing but the place and the body—will need to be supplemented by the head, so that one will have to count three and not just two. Here the stakes of materialism change. It is now necessary that the head be maintained in the unity of the place, that it not be made into an *other* place. The head must never be inscribed into an originary dualism, even though one must go up to three, even though the great temptation of the three (thought) is to count the two *elsewhere*. Here lies the text's crucial metaphysical tension.

These points are enumerated several times by Beckett in the text itself, which is marked by recapitulations. For example, on page 104:

> What it is the words it secretes say. What the so-said void. The so-said dim. The so-said shades. The so-said seat and germ of all.

We are presented here with the entirety of the constitutive thematic of *Worstward Ho.* "There is": What there is, is "what . . . the words it secretes say," under the imperative of saying; the question of being: "the so-said void" and "the so-said dim"; the question of the "there is" in the "there is," or the question of appearance: "The so-said shades." Finally, "the so-said seat and germ of all," the question of the head or skull, the question of thought.

Together, these questions make up what Beckett considers as the minimal *dispositif* that fixes a course—a "-ward" [*cap*]—for the "on" of saying. The minimal *dispositif*, the least *dispositif*, that is, the "worst" *dispositif* for a question to take place (we will see that the least and the worst amount to the same), for there to be an infinitesimal or minimal sense for any question whatever.

d) The Question and Its Conditions

What is a question? A question is what fixes the "-ward" for the "on" of saying. One will call "question" the fact that the navigation of the "on" has a -ward. And this -ward will be the worstward ho, the direction of the worst.

In order that there be a question—a worstward ho, that is—there must be a minimal *dispositif*, constituted precisely by the elements that we have just enumerated. From this point of view, *Worstward Ho* is itself a minimal text, that is, a text that establishes the elementary materials for any possible question in accordance with a method of drastic reduction. It is a text that tries not to introduce any useless or supernumerary element in defining the possibility of a question.

The first condition needed so that a minimal *dispositif* for a question can take place is without doubt that there be pure being, accompanied by its singular name: the void. But it is also necessary that there be the exposition of being, that is, not only being qua being, but being exposed according to its own being, or the phenomenality of the phenomenon. In other words, what is required is the possibility that something appear in its being. This possibility is not constituted by the void, which is instead the name of being qua being. The name of being qua possibility of appearance is "dim."[5]

The dim is being to the extent that a question can be formulated as to the being of being, that is, to the extent that being is exposed to the question qua reserve of being for appearance.

This is why there must be two names (void and dim) and not just one. For a question to be, being must have two names. Heidegger saw this, too, in his concepts of *Sein* and *Seiende*.

The second condition for a question is that there be thought. A skull-thought, let us call it. Skull-thought is an ill seeing and an ill saying or a clenched staring eye and an oozing of names. But, and this point is essential, the skull-thought is *itself* exposed. It is not subtracted from the exposition of being. It is not simply definable as that for which there is being—it participates in being as such, it is caught in its exposition. In Beckett's vocabulary, one will say that the head (seat and terminus of all) or the skull are *in* the dim. Or that skull-thought is the third shade. Or, again, that the skull-thought lets itself be counted in the uncountable dim.

Does this not leave us exposed to an infinite regress? If thought as such cobelongs with being, where is the thought of this cobelonging? From where is it said that the head is in the dim? It seems that we are on the edge of the necessity—if one can hazard this expression—of a metahead. One must count four, and then five, and so on to infinity.

The protocol of closure is given by the cogito. It is necessary to admit that the head is counted by the head, or that the head sees itself as head. Or again, that it is for the clenched staring eye that there is a clenched staring eye. Here lies the Cartesian thread running through Beckett's thought. Beckett never denied this thread, which is present from the beginning of his work, but in *Worstward Ho* it is identified as a kind of halting rule that alone allows that *for which* there is the dim also to be in the dim.

Finally, and still remaining within the register of the minimal conditions for a question, there must be—besides the "there is" and the skull-thought—inscriptions of shade in the dim.

Shades are ruled by three relations. First, that of the one or the two, or of the same and the other. In other terms, the relation of the kneeling one and the walking pair, taken, like Platonic categories, as figures of the same and the other. Second, that of the extremes of age, infancy, and senescence, extremes that also make it so that the pair is one. Third, the relation of the sexes, woman and man.

These are the constitutive relations of shades that populate the dim and infest the void.

A parenthesis: There is a point, only alluded to in *Worstward Ho*, which is nevertheless crucial. It is that, as we have seen, the sexes are without proof. More specifically, they are the only thing to be without proof. The fact that this shade turns out to be an old woman or an old man, this is always without proof while nevertheless being certain. This means that, for Beckett, the differentiation of the sexes is, at one and the same time, absolutely certain and absolutely beyond proof. This is why I can call it a pure disjunction.

Why a pure disjunction? It is certain that there is "woman" and there is "man"—in this case the old woman and the old man—but this certainty does not let itself be deduced or inferred on the basis of any particular predicative trait. It is therefore a prelinguistic certainty in the sense that it can be said, but that this saying does not in turn have any other saying as its source. It is a first saying. One can say that there are woman and man, but at no time can one infer this from another saying, and in particular not from a descriptive or empirical saying.

e) Being and Existence

Under these relations—of the one and the two, of the extremes of age, and of the sexes—the shades attest not to being, but to existence. What is existence, and what distinguishes it from being?

Existence is the generic attribute of what is capable of worsening. What can worsen exists. "Worsening" is the active modality of any exposition to the seeing of the clenched staring eye and to the oozing of words. This exposition is existence. Or, perhaps at a more fundamental level, what exists is what lets itself be encountered. Being exists when it is in the guise of the encounter.

Neither void nor dim designate something that can be encountered, because every encounter is under two conditions: on the one hand, that there be a possible interval of the void to section off what is encountered; on the other, that there be the dim, the exposition of everything that exposes itself. The shades are what lets itself be encountered. To let oneself be encountered and to worsen are one and the same thing, and it is this that designates the existence of shades. Void and dim—the names of being—do not exist.

Therefore, the minimal *dispositif* will also be referred to as follows: being, thought, existence. When one possesses the figures of being, thought, and existence, or the words for this *dispositif*, or, as Beckett would say, the words to "ill say" or "missay" it [6]—that is, when one possesses the minimal and experimental *dispositif* of saying—one can construct questions, one can set the -ward.

f) The Axiom of Saying

The text will thus organize itself by way of hypotheses concerning the

-ward, that is, the direction of thought. These hypotheses will concern what binds, unbinds, or affects the triad of dim being, shade existence, and skull-thought. *Worstward Ho* will treat the triad being/existence/thought under the categories of the void, of the same and the other, of the three, and of the seeing/saying complex.

Before formulating any hypotheses, one must seek support in a certain number of axioms that establish the primary bindings or unbindings. Almost the only axiom of *Worstward Ho*, which moreover generates its title, is an old axiom of Beckett's. It is by no means invented here and perhaps even constitutes one of his oldest axioms. This axiom goes: To say is to ill say.

It is necessary to understand fully that "to say is to ill say" establishes an essential identity. The essence of saying is ill saying. Ill saying is not a failure of saying, but precisely the contrary: All saying is, in its very existence as saying, an ill saying.

"Ill saying" is implicitly opposed to "well saying." What is "well saying"? "Well saying" is a hypothesis of adequation: The saying is adequate to the said. But Beckett's fundamental thesis is that the saying that is adequate to the said suppresses saying. Saying is a free saying, and in particular an artistic saying, only to the extent that it does not coalesce with the said, to the extent that it is not subject to the authority of the said. Saying is under the imperative of saying, it is under the imperative of the "on," and is not constrained by the said.

If there is no adequation, if the saying is not prescribed by "what is said," but governed only by saying, then ill saying is the free essence of saying or the affirmation of the prescriptive autonomy of saying. One says in order to ill say. The apex of saying—which is poetic or artistic saying—is then precisely the controlled regulation of ill saying, what brings the prescriptive autonomy of saying to its culmination.

When reading in Beckett terms such as "ill saying," "failure," and so on, it is necessary to keep all of this well in mind. Were we dealing with an empiricist doctrine of language according to which language sticks to things with various degrees of adherence, this would arouse no interest. Moreover, the text itself would be impossible. The text functions only from the moment that one hears in the expressions "fail" or "missay" the self-affirmation of the prescription of saying as governed by its own rule. Beckett clearly indicates this from the start:

Say for be said. Missaid. From now say for be missaid. (89)

g) The Temptation

The strict consequence of all this is that the norm of saying is called "failure." Of course, the fact that failure provides the norm of saying arouses a fallacious hope within the subject, a hope that Beckett identifies perfectly: the hope of a maximal failure, of an absolute failure that would have the merit of turning you off both language and saying, once and for all. This is the shameful temptation, the temptation of subtracting oneself from the imperative of saying. The temptation to have done with the "on," no longer to suffer the intolerable prescription of ill saying.

Since well saying is impossible, the only hope lies in betrayal: To attain a failure so complete it would elicit a total abandonment of the prescription itself, a relinquishment of saying and of language. This would mean the return to the void—to be void or emptied, emptied of all prescription. In the end, the temptation is to cease to exist in order to be. In this form of failure one returns to the void, to pure being. This is what we could call the mystical temptation, in the sense in which it appears in Wittgenstein, in the last proposition of the *Tractatus*. To reach the point at which, since it is impossible to speak, one can only remain silent. To reach the point at which the awareness that it is impossible to say "it," that is, the awareness that "it" has failed absolutely, firmly places you under the sway of an imperative that is no longer the imperative of saying, but the imperative of silence.

In Beckett's vocabulary this is called "going." Going where? Well, going away from humanity. In truth, like Rimbaud, Beckett thinks that one never leaves. He recognizes absolutely the temptation of leaving humanity, the temptation of failing both language and saying to the point of disgust. To leave existence once and for all, to return to being. But Beckett corrects and ultimately rejects this possibility.

Here is a text in which he evokes the hypothesis of an access to going and to the void by means an excess of failure, an excess of failure that would be indistinguishable from the absolute success of saying:

> Try again. Fail again. Better again. Or better worse. Fail worse again. Still worse again. Till sick for good. Throw up for good. Go for good. Where neither for good. Good and all. (90)

This is the temptation: to go where all shade is gone, where nothing is any longer exposed to the imperative of saying.

But in numerous passages, further on in the text, this temptation will be challenged, revoked, prohibited. For example on page 110, where the idea of the "better worse more" is declared to be inconceivable:

> Back unsay better worse by no stretch more. If more dim less light then better worse more dim. Unsaid then better worse by no stretch more. Better worse may no less than less be more. Better worse what? The say? The said? Same thing. Same nothing. Same all but nothing.

The fundamental point is that the "throw up for good, good and all" does not exist, because every "same nothing" is really a "same all but nothing." The hypothesis of a radical departure that would subtract us from the humanity of the imperative—the essential temptation at work in the prescription of silence—cannot succeed for ontological reasons. The "same nothing" is really always a "same all but nothing," or a "same almost nothing," but never a "same nothing" as such. Thus, there are never sufficient grounds for subtracting oneself from the imperative of saying in the name either of the advent of a pure "nothing" or of absolute failure.

h) The Laws of Worsening

From this point onward, the fundamental law that governs the text is that the worst that language is capable of—the worsening—never lets itself be captured by the nothing. One is always in the "same all but nothing," but never at the point of the "go for good," where a capture by the nothing would take place. This would be a nothing that is neither void nor dim, but the pure and simple abolition of the prescription of saying.

We must therefore maintain the following: Language partakes exclusively of the capacity of the least. It does not partake of the capacity of the nothing. It has, as Beckett will say, "leastening words". One has words that leasten, and these words that leasten are those thanks to which one can hold to the worstward ho, that is, the direction of a centering of failure.

Between Mallarmé's "allusive, never direct words" and Beckett's "leastening words" the filiation is evident. To approach the thing that is to be said in the awareness that it cannot be said under the guarantee of saying—or of the thing—leads to a radical autonomization of the prescription of saying. This free saying can never be direct, or, according to Beckett's vocabulary, it is a saying that leastens, that worsens.

In other words, language can expect the minimum of the best worse, but not its abolition. Here is the essential text, the one in which the expression "leastening words" also appears:

Worse less. By no stretch more. Worse for want of better less. Less best. No. Naught best. Best worse. No. Not best worse. Naught not best worse. Less best worse. No. Least. Least best worse. Least never to be naught. Never to naught be brought. Never by naught be nulled. Unnullable least. Say that best worse. With leastening words say least best worse. For want of worser worst. Unlessenable least best worse. (106)

"Least never to be naught" is the law of worsening. "Say that best worse" is the "unnullable least." The "unlessenable least best worse" can never be confused with abolition pure and simple or with the nothing. This means that "one must remain silent," in Wittgenstein's sense, is impracticable. We must hold the worstward ho. *Worstward Ho*: The title is an imperative, and not simply a description.

The imperative of saying thus takes the guise of a constant reprise; it belongs to the regime of the attempt, of effort, of work. The book itself will try to worsen everything that offers itself up to the oozing of words. A considerable amount of the text is devoted to what could be called experiments in "worsening." *Worstward Ho* is a protocol of worsening, presented as a figure of the self-affirmation of the prescription of saying. Worsening is a sovereign procedure of naming in the excess of failure. It is the same as arousing thought by "never direct allusive words" and carries with it the same impassable proximity to nothingness as Mallarmé's poetry.

Worsening, which is the exercise of language in its artistic tension, takes place through two contradictory operations. What in fact is worsening? It is the exercise of the sovereignty of saying with respect to the shades. Therefore, it is both saying more about them and restricting what is said. This is why the operations are contradictory. Worsening is saying more about less. More words to better leasten.

Whence the paradoxical aspect of worsening, which is really the substance of the text. In order to leasten "what is said" so that—with regard to this purging [*épuration*]—failure may become more manifest, it will be necessary to introduce new words. These words are not additions—one does not add, one does not make sums—but one must say more in order to leasten, and thus one must say more in order to subtract. Here lies the constitutive operation of language. To worsen is to advance the "saying more" in order to leasten.

i) Exercises in Worsening

The text lavishly multiplies worsening exercises over the entire phenomenal field of shades, over the configuration of generic humanity. These can be briefly categorized as follows:

—Worsening the one, or, worsening the kneeling woman;

—Worsening the two, or, worsening the pair of the old man and the child;

—Worsening the head, or, worsening the eyes, the oozing brain, and the skull.

These are the three shades that constitute the phenomenal determinations of shade.

Worsening the one: This is the exercise that occupies page 99:

> First one. First try fail better one. Something there badly not wrong. Not that as it is it is not bad. The no face bad. The no hands bad. The no—. Enough. A pox on bad. Mere bad. Way for worse. Pending worse still. First worse. Mere worse. Pending worse still. Add a—. Add? Never. Bow it down. Be it bowed down. Deep down. Head in hat gone. More back gone. Greatcoat cut off higher. Nothing from pelvis down. Nothing but bowed back. Topless baseless hindtrunk. Dim black. On unseen knees. In the dim void. Better worse so. Pending worse still.

The deployment of names that marks out this first shade with a great number of subtractive attributes is, at the same time, its leastening or reduction. Its reduction to what? Well, to what should be named a *mark of the one* [*un trait d'un*], a mark that would give the shade with nothing else besides. The words demanded for this mark are "bowed back." A simple curve. Nothing but a curve, such would be the ideality of the "worse still," knowing that more words are needed in order to make such a curve arise, because words alone operate the leastening. Thus, an operation of nominal overabundance—overabundance always being relative in Beckett—aims here at an essential leastening.

This is the law of worsening: One cuts the legs, the head, the coat, one cuts all that one can, but each cut is in truth centered on the advent—by way of supplementary subtractive details—of a pure mark. One must supplement so as to purge the last mark of failure.

And now the worsening exercise of the two:

> Next two. From bad to worsen. Try worsen. From merely bad. Add—. Add?

Never. The boots. Better worse bootless. Bare heels. Now the two right. Now the two left. Left right left right on. Barefoot unreceding on. Better worse so. A little better worse than nothing so. (100)

The boots—there aren't many names like "boots" in this piece, whose texture is extremely abstract. When there are such names, it is a sure sign that we are dealing with a risky operation. In a moment we will see this with a concrete and essential word, the irruption of "cemetery." Nevertheless, the boot, which appears all of a sudden, is there only in order to be crossed out, erased: "The boots. Better worse bootless."

A part of things is only given so as to fail, to be crossed out. It comes to the surface of the text only so as to be subtracted. Here lies the contradictory nature of the operation. The logic of worsening, which is the logic of the sovereignty of language, equates addition and subtraction. Mallarmé did not proceed otherwise. Mallarmé, for whom the very act of the poem consists in bringing about the emergence of an object (swan, star, rose ...), an object whose arrival imposes its own termination. Beckett's "boot" is the support-term of such an act.

Finally, worsening the head. This passage concerns the eyes (recall that the skull is composed of eyes on a brain):

The eyes. Time to try worsen. Somehow try worsen. Unclench. Say staring open. All white and pupil. Dim white. White? No. All pupil. Dim black holes. Unwavering gaping. Be they so said. With worsening words. From now so. Better than nothing so bettered for the worse. (103)

The logic of the writing in this passage is altogether typical. On the basis of the syntagm "clenched staring"—whose meaning I've already discussed—we have the attempt at an opening. We will pass from "clenched staring" to "staring open," which is a semantically homogeneous datum. "Open" will in turn give us white, and white will be terminated, giving us black. This is the immediate chain. We pass from clenched to open, from open to white, and then white is crossed out in favor of black. The outcome of the operation—the operation of worsening—is that in place of "clenched staring" we will have "black holes" and that, from now on, when it will be a question of eyes, it will no longer even be in terms of the word "eyes"—Beckett will simply mention two black holes.

Note that the open and the black emerge only within the sequence of the operation in order to pass from eyes to black holes and that this operation of worsening aims at ridding us of the word "eyes"—too descriptive, too empirical, and too singular—so as to lead us, by way of diagonal worsening and deletion, to the simple acceptance of black holes as blind seats of visibility. The eye as such is abolished. From this point onward, there is only a pure seeing linked to a hole, and this pure seeing linked to a hole is constructed by means of the abolition of the eye with the (supplementary and exemplary) mediation of the open and the white.

j) Holding Worstward

Worsening is a labor, an inventive and arduous effectuation of the imperative of saying. Being an effort, holding to the worstward ho demands courage.

Where does the courage of effort come from? I think this is a very important question, because it is in general the question of knowing where the courage of holding to any procedure of truth comes from. The question is ultimately the following: Where does the courage of truth come from?

For Beckett, the courage of truth could not come from the idea that we will be repaid by silence or by a successful coincidence with being as such. We have seen this already: There will be no termination of saying, no advent of the void as such. The *on* cannot be effaced.

So, where does courage come from? For Beckett, courage comes from the fact that words have the tendency to ring true. An extreme tension, which perhaps constitutes Beckett's vocation as a writer, results from the fact that courage pertains to a quality of words that is contrary to their use in worsening. There is something like an *aura* of correspondence in words from which (paradoxically) we draw the courage to break with correspondence itself, that is, to hold worstward.

The courage of effort is always drawn out against its own destination. Let us call this "the torsion of saying": The courage of the continuation of effort is drawn from words themselves, but from words taken against their genuine destination, which is to worsen.

Effort—in this case, artistic or poetic effort—is a barren work on language undertaken in order to submit language to the exercises of worsening. But this barren effort draws its energy from a fortunate disposition of language: a sort of phantom of correspondence that haunts language to which one returns as if it were the possible place in which to draw from language itself, but wholly against the grain of its destination, the courage of its treatment. In *Worstward Ho*, this tension gives rise to some very beautiful passages. Here is the first:

> The words too whosesoever. What room for worse! How almost true they sometimes almost ring! How wanting in inanity! Say the night is young alas and take heart. Or better worse say still a watch of night alas to come. A rest of last watch to come. And take heart [*Et prendre courage*] (99)

It is to the extent that one can say something that rings almost true—that one can say what in the poem is "like" the true, and take heart—that one holds worstward. "Say the night is young alas and take heart." How magnificent! Here is a variation on the theme:

> What words for what then? How almost they still ring. As somehow from some soft of mind they ooze. From it in it ooze. How all but uninane. To last unlessenable least how loath to leasten. For then in utmost dim to unutter leastmost all. (107)

Everything here shows to what extent one is "loath to leasten," to what extent this effort is barren. One loathes to leasten because words are "all but uninane," because the word sounds true, because it rings clear and it is from the word that we take heart, that we draw our courage. But taking heart for what? Well, precisely in order to ill say; to challenge the illusion that it rings true, the illusion that summons us to courage. The torsion of saying is thus both what clarifies the barrenness of effort (one must overcome, toward the worst, the clarity of words) and the courage with which we treat this barrenness.

Nevertheless, there is another reason why holding worstward proves difficult: Being as such resists, being rebels against the logic of the worst. As worsening comes to be exercised upon the shades, one reaches the edge of the dim, the edge of the void, and there to continue to worsen becomes more and more difficult. As if the experience of being were witness not to an impasse of worsening, but to a difficulty, to a growing effort—ever more exhausting—in this worsening.

When one is led to the edge of being by a barren and attentive exercise in the worsening of appearances, a sort of invariance comes to confound saying, exposing it to an experience of suffering—as if the imperative of saying encountered here what is furthest away from it, or most indifferent. This will be said in two ways: according to the dim or according to the

void. This relation between the dim, the void, and the imperative of saying brings us to the core of our ontological questions.

Let us recall that dim is the name of what exposes being. It follows from
this that the dim can never be a total darkness, a darkness that the imperative of saying desires as its own impossibility. The imperative of saying,
which desires the leastmost, is polarized by the idea that the dim could become the obscure, the absolutely dark. The text makes several hypotheses
concerning how this desire can be satisfied. But these hypotheses are ultimately rejected, for there is always a minimal exposition of being. The being of void being is to expose itself as dim; in other words, the being of being is to expose itself, and exposition rules out the absoluteness of the dark
or obscure. Even if one can lessen the exposition, one can never attain the
obscure as such. Of the dim, it will be said that it is an "unworsenable
worst":

> So leastward on. So long as dim still. Dim undimmed. Or dimmed to dimmer
> still [*plus obscur encore*]. To dimmost dim. Leastmost in dimmost dim. Utmost
> dim. Leastmost in utmost dim. Unworsenable worst. (107)

Thought can move in the leastmost, in the utmost dim, but it has no
access to the obscure as such. There is always a lesser least—so let us state
the fundamental axiom once again: "least never to be naught." The argument is simple: Because the dim, which is the exposition of being, is a
condition of the worstward ho—what exposes it to saying—it can never
be entirely given over to it. We may go worstward, but we can never go
"naughtward" [*Nous ne pouvons mettre le cap sur le néant, seulement sur le
pire*]. There can be no "naughtward" precisely because the dim is a condition of the -ward. Thus, one can argue for the quasi-obscure, the almost
obscure, but the dim in its being remains dim. Ultimately, the dim resists
worsening.

k) The Unworsenable Void

The void is given in experience. It is given in the interval of shades within
the dim. It is what separates. In fact, the void is the ground [*fond*] of being, but in its exposition it is a pure gap [*écart*]. With respect to the shades
or the pair, Beckett will say: "vast of void atween." Such is the figure in
which the void is given.

The worsening aims to get closer to the void as such, no longer to have the void in its mere dimension of interval, but the void as void—being as retracted from its exposition. But if the void is subtracted from its own exposition, it can no longer be the correlate of the process of worsening, because the process of worsening works only on shades and on their void intervals. So that the void "in itself" cannot be worked upon in accordance with the laws of worsening. You can vary the intervals, but the void as void remains radically unworsenable. Now, if it is radically unworsenable, it means that it cannot even be ill said. This point is a very subtle one. The void "in itself" is what cannot be ill said. This is its definition. The void *cannot but be said.* In it, the saying and the said coincide, which prohibits ill saying. Such a coincidence finds its reason in the fact that the void itself is nothing but its own name. Of the void "in itself" you have nothing but the name. Within Beckett's text this is expressly formulated as follows:

The void. How try say? How try fail? No try no fail. Say only— (96)

That the void is subtracted from ill saying means that there is no art of the void. The void is subtracted from what within language suggests an art: the logic of worsening. When you say "the void," you have said all that can be said, and you possess no process that could elicit the metamorphosis of this saying. In other words, there is no metaphor for the void.

In the subjective register, the void, being but a name, arouses only the desire for its disappearance. In the skull, the void arouses not the process of worsening—which is impossible in its regard—but the absolute impatience of this pure name, the desire that the void be exposed as such, annihilated, something that is nevertheless impossible.

As soon as one touches upon a void that is not an interval, upon the void "in itself," one enters what in Beckett constitutes the figure of an ontological desire that is subtracted from the imperative of saying: the fusion of the nothingness of the void, on the one hand, and the dim, on the other. It will also be remarked that, in a manner resembling the functioning of drives, the name of the void sets off a desire for disappearance, but that this desire for disappearance is without object, for there is here nothing but a name. The void will always counter any process of disappearance with the fact that it is effectively subtracted from worsening. This subtraction results from a property of the void, which is that in it, the "maximum" and the "almost" are the same thing. Let us note that this is not the case with the dim, so that the two names of being do not function in the same way. The dim can be dimmost, leastmost dimmost. The void cannot. The void cannot but be said, seized as pure name, and subtracted from every principle of variability, and therefore of metaphor or metamorphosis, because within it, the "maximum" and the "almost" coincide absolutely. Here then is the great passage on the void:

> All save void. No. Void too. Unworsenable void. Never less. Never more. Never since first said never unsaid never worse said never not gnawing to be gone.
> Say child gone. . . (113)

"Say child gone": Beckett attempts to approach the question at an angle. The unworsenable void cannot disappear, but if, for example, one makes a shade disappear, since one is dealing with a shade-infested void, perhaps a greater void will ensue. This growth would deliver the void over to the process of language. It is this experiment that the continuation of the text describes:

> Say child gone. As good as gone. From the void. From the stare. Void then not that much more? Say old man gone. Old woman gone. As good as gone. Void then not that much more again? No. Void most when almost. Worst when almost. Less then? All shades as good as gone. If then not that much more then that much less then? Less worse then? Enough. A pox on void. Unmoreable unlessable unworseable evermost almost void. (113)

The experiment, as one can see, fails. The void qua pure nomination remains radically unworsenable, and thus unsayable.

l) Appearing and Disappearing. Movement

Together with the supposed movements of appearance and disappearance, the argument tied to the void summons all of the Platonic supreme ideas. We have being, which is the void and the dim; the same, which is the one-woman; the other, which is the old man / child two. The question is that of knowing what becomes of movement and rest, the last two categories in the five primordial genera of *The Sophist*.

The question of movement and rest presents itself in the form of two interrogations: What can disappear? And: What can change?

There is an absolutely essential thesis that says that absolute disappearance is the disappearance of the dim. If one asks: What can disappear *absolutely*? The response is: The dim. For example:

> On back to unsay void can go [*disparition du vide*].[As I've already noted, the disappearance of the void is subordinated to the disappearance of the dim.—AB.] Void cannot go. Save dim go. Then all go. All not already gone. Till dim back. Then all back. All not still gone. The one can go. The twain can go. Dim can go. Void cannot go. Save dim go. Then all go. (97)

There always remains the possible hypothesis of an absolute disappearance that would present itself as the disappearance of exposition itself and therefore as the disappearance of the dim. But one must not forget that this hypothesis is beyond saying, that the imperative of saying has nothing to do with the possibility of the disappearance of the dim. Hence the disappearance of the dim, like its reappearance, is an abstract hypothesis that can be formulated, but that does not give rise to any experience whatsoever. There is a horizon of absolute disappearance, thinkable in the statement "dim can go." Nevertheless, this statement remains indifferent to the entire protocol of the text.

The problem will therefore center upon the appearance and disappearance of shades. This is a problem of an altogether different order, which is associated to the question of thought. On the contrary, the hypothesis of the disappearance dim is beyond saying and beyond thought. More generally, this new problem is to do with the movement of shades.

The investigation of this point is very complex, and I will limit myself here to presenting my conclusions alone.

First, the one is not capable of movement. The figure of the old woman, which is the mark of the One, will certainly be termed "stooped" and then "kneeling," all of which seems to express change. But the crucial proviso is that we are dealing here only with prescriptions of saying, rules of the worst, and never with a movement proper. It is not true that the one stoops or kneels. The text always states that *one* [*on*] will say kneeling, sunk, and so on. All this is prescribed by the logic of lessening within worsening, but does not indicate any proper capacity of the one [*l'un*] to any sort of movement.

The first thesis is therefore Parmenidean: What is counted as one, insofar as it is counted only as one, remains indifferent to movement.

Second statement: Thought (the head, the skull) is incapable of disappearing. There are a number of texts concerning this point. Here is one:

The head. Ask not if it can go. Say no. Unasking no. It cannot go. Save dim go. Then all go. Oh dim go. Go for good. All for good. Good and all. (98)

This "Oh dim go" remains without effect. As we've seen, you can always say "Oh dim go," the dim does not care in the least.

What is important for us then is that the head is incapable of disappearing, save of course the dim go, but then all go.

Consequently, we must note that the head has the same status as the void when it comes to the question of disappearance. This is exactly Parmenides' maxim: "It is the same to think and to be." Parmenides designates the essential ontological pairing of thought and being. And concerning the question of disappearance—which is the very test or ordeal of being—*Worstward Ho* declares that the skull and the void are under the same sign.

This means that ultimately only the other, or the two, supports movement: This is the third thesis.

This is a classical thesis, a Greek thesis. There is no movement but of the pair, that is, of the old man and the child. It is they who walk, who plod on. This is the idea that movement qua alteration is consubstantially linked to the other. But what is significant is that this movement is in a certain sense immobile. When speaking of the old man and the child—this is a veritable leitmotif—the text will constantly say:

Plod on and never recede. (93)

There is movement, but there is an internal immobility to this movement. They plod on and never recede. What does this mean? Of course, this means that there is movement (they plod on) but that there is only one situation of being, that there is only one ontological situation. One will also say: There is but one place. This is what is declared very early on by the maxim:

No place but the one. (92)

There is but one place, or one universe. There is only one figure of being, not two. For the pair effectively to recede, for it to recede in going, there would have to be an "other" place, the pair would have to be able to *pass* into another place. But there is no other place: "No place but the one." In other words, there is no duality in being. Being is One in its localization. This is why movement must always be recognized, but, at the same time, must be grasped as relative because it does not allow us to leave the unity of the place. This is what is confirmed by the pair.

m) Love

This immobile migration, which is that of the two, is deeply marked by Beckett's conception of love. Here it is the old man and the child, but it matters little. What we have is the maxim of the two, and, in that prodigious text on love that is *Enough*, Beckett presents us with the two of love as a sort of migration, which is at the same time a migration unto oneself. Such is the essence of love. The migration does not make one pass from one place to another. Instead, it is a delocalization internal to the place, and this immanent delocalization finds its paradigm in the two of love. This explains why the passages on the old man and the child are marked by a muted emotion that is very particular to *Worstward Ho*: The immobile migration designates what could be called the spatiality of love.

Here is one of these texts in which a powerful and abstract tenderness—echoing *Enough*—can be heard:

> Hand in hand with equal plod they go. In the free hands—no. Free empty hands. Backs turned both bowed with equal plod they go. The child hand raised to reach the holding hand. Hold the old holding hand. Hold and be held. Plod on and never recede. Slowly with never a pause plod on and never recede. Backs turned. Both bowed. Joined by held holding hands. Plod on as one. One shade. Another shade. (93)

n) Appearing and Disappearing. Change. The Skull

A hypothesis accessible to the skull would be that the shades—between a disappearance and a reappearance—have been modified. This hypothesis is evoked and worked through, but it is expressly presented as a hypothesis of saying:

> They fade [*disparaissent*]. Now the one. Now the twain. Now both. Fade back [*réapparaissent*]. Now the one. Now the twain. Now both. Fade? No. Sudden go. Sudden back. Now the one. Now the twain. Now both.
> Unchanged? Sudden back unchanged? Yes. Say yes. Each time unchanged. Somehow unchanged. Till no. Till say no. Sudden back unchanged. Somehow changed. Each time somehow changed. (94)

That there can be real changes, that is, changes caught between appearance and disappearance, is not a hypothesis liable to affect the being of a shade. Rather, it is a hypothesis that the prescription of saying might formulate. It is somewhat like above with "Oh dim go," or when one says "kneeling," "stooped," and so on. It is necessary to distinguish what is an attribute of the shade itself from the hypothetical variation it can be submitted to by the prescription of saying.

In the end, with regard to shades of type one (the woman) and type two (the old man and the child), only the immobile migration of the pair bears witness to a movement.

Thus we are finally led to the question of the changes of the type three shade, the skull, the skull from which words ooze, the skull from which the prescription of saying oozes. At this juncture, there clearly intervenes the halting point of which we spoke above: the structure of the cogito. Every modification, disappearance, reappearance, or alteration of the skull is blocked by the fact that the skull must be represented as what seizes itself in the dim.

Therefore we cannot presume that everything has disappeared in the skull. The hypothesis of radical doubt, which would affect the shades with a total disappearance—subjected to the prescription to be made by the skull—cannot be maintained for the same reasons that force Cartesian radical doubt to impose limits upon itself. Here is the passage in question:

> In the skull all gone [*disparu*]. All? No. All cannot go. Till dim go. Say then but the two gone. In the skull one and two gone. From the void. From the stare. In the skull all save the skull gone. The stare. Alone in the dim void. Alone to be seen. Dimly seen. In the skull the skull alone to be seen. The staring eyes. Dimly seen. By the staring eyes. (102)

The hypothesis of the disappearance of the shades, based on the fact that they would have gone from the skull—and thus that they would no longer be of the order of seeing or of ill seeing—does not entail the disappearance of the all, the "all go." In particular, it does not entail the disappearance of all the shades, because the skull, which itself is a shade, cannot itself disappear or "go."

The Cartesian matrix is necessarily stated as follows: "In the skull all save the skull gone." I think, therefore I am a shade in the dim. The skull is the shade-subject and cannot disappear—it cannot "go."

0) Of the Subject as Skull. Will, Pain, Joy

The subject as skull is fundamentally reducible to saying and seeing. The skull brings together staring eyes and a brain. But there are, as in Descartes, other affections. In particular, there are the will, pain, and joy, all of whose places are assigned in the text. Each of these affections will be studied in accordance with the method of worsening, that is, in their essential "unlessenable least."

What is the essential unlessenable least of the will? It is the will given in its ultimate form, which is to will the nonwill or to will that there shall be no more willing, that is, to will itself as nonwill. In Beckett's own words this is the "longing that vain longing go":

> Longing the so-said mind long lost to longing. The so-missaid. So far so-missaid. Dint of long longing lost to longing. Long vain longing. And longing still. Faintly longing still. Faintly vainly longing still. For fainter still. For faintest. Faintly vainly longing for the least of longing. Unlessenable least of longing. Unstillable vain last of longing still.
> Longing that all go [*que tout disparaisse*]. Dim go. Void go. Longing go. Vain longing that vain longing go. (109)

Many comments could be made regarding the correlations between this passage and the canonical doctrines of will. We could say that willing is shaped by the imperative of saying and that the "all go"—the will that the "vain longing that vain longing go" itself go or disappear—is the irreducible trace of will, or that the will, as the imperative of saying, cannot but go on.

Pain is of the body (while joy comes from words). In the body, pain is what provokes movement, and this is what makes it the first witness of the remains of mind. Pain is the bodily proof that there are remains of mind, inasmuch as it is what arouses the shades to movement:

> It stands. What? Yes. Say it stands. Had to up in the end and stand. Say bones. No bones but say bones. Say ground. No ground but say ground. So as to say pain. No mind and pain? Say yes that the bones may pain till no choice but stand. Somehow up and stand. Or better worse remains. Say remains of mind where none to permit of pain. Pain of bones till no choice but up and stand. Somehow up. Somehow stand. Remains of mind where none for the sake of pain. Here of bones. Other examples if needs must. Of pain. Relief from. Change of. (90)

Joy, in the end, is on the side of words. To rejoice is to rejoice that there are so few words to say what there is to say. Joy is always the joy of the poverty of words. The mark of the state of joy or of rejoicing—of what rejoices—is that there are exceedingly few words to say it. Upon reflection, this is entirely true. Extreme joy is precisely what possesses few or no words to speak itself. Whence the fact that in the figure of the declaration of love there is nothing to say but "I love you"—an extremely meager statement, because it finds itself in the element of joy.

I am thinking, in Richard Strauss's *Elektra*, of the scene of the recognition of Orestes by Elektra in which Elektra sings a very violent "Orestes!" and the music is suddenly paralyzed. Here is a musical passage in fortissimo, but one that is absolutely formless and rather lengthy. I have always liked that quite a lot. It is as if an unspeakable and extreme joy were musically presented in the self-paralysis of the music, as if its internal melodic configuration (which later on will present itself, over and over again, in saccharine waltzes) were stricken by powerlessness: Here is a moment of "rejoicing" understood as an impoverished disposition of naming.

Beckett says this very clearly. It is evidently linked to the fact that there are poor remains of mind and poor words for these poor remains:

> Remains of mind then still. Enough still. Somewhose somewhere somehow enough still. No mind and words? Even such words. So enough still. Just enough still to joy. Joy! Just enough still to joy that only they. Only! (104)

So much for the subjective faculties other than seeing and saying, and above all the three main ones (will, pain, joy). All things considered, what we have here is a classical doctrine of the passions.

p) How Can a Subject Be Thought?

Given what we have just said, if we wish to proceed in the study of the subject, we must do so subtractively. Fundamentally, Beckett's method is like Husserl's epoché turned upside down. Husserl's epoché consists in subtracting the thesis of the world, in subtracting the "there is," in order then to turn toward the movement or the pure flux of the interiority that is directed at this "there is." Husserl's lineage originates in Cartesian doubt. The thetic character of the universe of the intentional operations of consciousness is retracted in order to try to apprehend the conscious structure that governs these operations, independently of any thesis concerning the world.

Beckett's method is precisely the opposite: It is a question of subtracting or suspending the subject so as to see what then happens to being. The hypothesis of a seeing without words will be forwarded. The hypothesis of words without seeing will also be made, together with a hypothesis of a disappearance of words. And it will be noted there is then a better seen [*du mieux vu*]. Here is one of the protocols of this experiment:

> Blanks for when words gone. When nohow on. Then all seen as only then. Undimmed. All undimmed that words dim. All so seen unsaid. No ooze then. No trace on soft when from it ooze again. In it ooze again. Ooze alone for seen as seen with ooze. Dimmed. No ooze for seen undimmed. For when nohow on. No ooze for when ooze gone. (112)

Here it would be necessary to explain the text in greater detail. We are dealing with a protocol of seeing that remains undimmed when the hypothesis of a disappearance of words is made, the hypothesis of the real end of the imperative of saying. Like Husserl's epoché, this is a pure abstract hypothesis, as well as an untenable hypothesis, one that is actually impracticable. In this hypothesis, some light is shed on being. The inverse experiment can also be carried out: subtracting sight and then asking oneself what is the destiny of an ill saying that is disconnected from seeing, from ill seeing.

I shall not develop these experiments any further. Ultimately, if we recapitulate our argument about the question of disappearance, we can obtain three propositions.

First of all, the void is unworsenable once it is caught in the exposition of the dim. This means that there is no experience of being, only a name of being. A name commands a saying, but an experience is an ill saying and not a saying proper.

Secondly, the skull or subject cannot *really* be subtracted from seeing and saying, it can be subtracted only in formal experiments [*expériences*], in particular because for itself it is always "not gone."

Finally, the shades—that is, the same and the other—are worsenable (from the point of view of the skull) and are therefore objects of experience, of artistic exposition.

Here is what is exposed, said, and outlined in the text, together with a host of other things. In *Worstward Ho*, there is an entire doctrine of time, of space, of variations . . . we could go on.

At least until page 115. Because from this point onward, something else happens whose complexity is such that long analyses would still be required in order to get to the bottom of it. Let me simply indicate the essential points.

q) The Event

Until page 115, we remain within the parameters of the minimal *dispositif* that links being, existence, and thought. It is at this point that we witness the production of an event in the strict sense—a discontinuity, an event prepared by what Beckett calls a *last state*. The last state is *grosso modo* what we have just described: It is the last state as the last state of the state, the last state of the saying of the state of things. This state is seized by the impossibility of annihilation—"save dim go," which remains a hypothesis beyond saying.

The event—of whose trajectory we shall have to say more—will arrange or expose an imperative of saying reduced ("leastened") to the statement of its own cessation. The conditions will be modified in and by the event in such a way that the content of the "on" will be strictly limited to the "nohow on." What will remain to be said will simply be that there is nothing more to be said. And thus we shall have a saying that has reached an absolutely maximal degree of purification.

Everything begins with the recapitulation of the last state:

> Same stoop for all. Same vasts apart. Such last state. Latest state. Till somehow less in vain. Worse in vain. All gnawing to be naught. Never to be naught. (115)

The last or latest state seals the process of worsening as interminable. Its maxim is: "Worse in vain." But once the recapitulation is complete, there brusquely occurs—in a moment introduced by "sudden"—a sort of distancing of this state to a limit position, which is like its absolute retreat into the interior of language. As if everything that had been said, by being able to be said in its last state, suddenly found itself at an infinitesimal distance from the imperative of language.

It must be said that this movement is absolutely parallel to the irruption of the Constellation at the end of Mallarmé's *Coup de dés*. In my view, the analogy is a conscious one—we shall see why. In this moment when there is nothing more to say but "behold the state of things, the things of being" (which Mallarmé says in the form: "Nothing has taken place but the place")—when one thinks that the text will stop there, that this maxim represents the last word on what the imperative of saying is capable of—it is as though a kind of addition took place. This addition is sudden, abrupt, in rupture, and takes place on a scene situated at a remove from the one at hand, a scene in which a metamorphosis of exposition is presented—a sidereal metamorphosis, or a "siderealization" [*sidération*]. It is not a question of the disappearance of the dim, but of a retreat of being to its very limit. Just as in Mallarmé the question of the dice throw results in the appearance of the Great Bear, likewise, what was counted in the dim will here be fixed in pinholes—a closely related metaphor. Here is the passage introduced by the clause of rupture, "Enough":

> Enough. Sudden enough. Sudden all far. No move and sudden all far. All least. Three pins. One pinhole. In dimmost dim. Vasts apart. At bounds of boundless void. Whence no farther. Best worse no farther. Nohow less. Nohow worse. Nohow naught. Nohow on.
>
> Said nohow on. (116)

I would simply like to insist upon a few points.

The intratextual, evental character of this limit disposition is marked by the fact that the "sudden" is devoid of movement: "Sudden all far. No move and sudden all far." Therefore it is not a change, but a separation. It is another scene, doubling the scene that was primordially established.

Second—making me think that the Mallarméan configuration is conscious—there is the passage: "Vasts apart. At bounds of boundless void." This sounds very close to "on high perhaps, as far as place can fuse with the beyond . . . a constellation." [7] I am absolutely convinced that Beckett's three pins and Mallarmé's seven stars are the same thing.

For thought, they are in fact the same thing: At the moment in which there is nothing more to say but the stable figure of being, there emerges, in a suddenness that amounts to a grace without concept, an overall configuration [*configuration d'ensemble*] in which one will be able to say "nohow on." Not an "on" ordained or prescribed to the shades, but simply "nohow on"—the "on" of saying reduced, or leastened, to the purity of its possible cessation.

However, the configuration of "possible saying" is no longer a state of being, an exercise in worsening. It is an event creating an *afar*. It is an incalculable distancing. From the point of view of the poetics of the text, we would need to demonstrate that this evental configuration—this "sudden"—is aesthetically or poetically prepared by a specific figure. In Mallarmé, the Constellation is prepared by the figure of the master, drowning himself on the surface of the sea. In Beckett, this figural preparation, which deserves to be admired, consists in the altogether unpredictable metamorphosis of the one-woman into the gravestone, in a passage whose imagery of discontinuity should alert us. A page before the event at the limits, we find the following:

> Nothing and yet a woman. Old and yet old. On unseen knees. Stooped as loving memory some old gravestones stoop. In that old graveyard. Names gone and when to when. Stoop mute over the graves of none. (115)

This passage is absolutely singular and paradoxical in relation to what we have argued hitherto. First of all, because it makes a metaphor emerge with regard to the shades. The one-woman, the stoop of the one-woman, literally becomes a gravestone. And on the stoop of this gravestone, the subject is now given only in the erasure of its name, in the crossing out of its name and date of existence.

It could be said that it is on the background of these "graves of none," on this new stoop, that the "enough" indicates the possibility of the event. The stoop opens onto the sudden. The anonymous tomb opens onto the astral pin.

In *Coup de dés*, it is because the element of the place has managed to metamorphose into something other than itself that the evental rupture of the Constellation is possible.

In *Worstward Ho*, we have a grave—the old woman herself has become a grave, a one-grave. Likewise, in Mallarmé's poem, we have the foam becoming vessel and, in so doing, calling forth the vessel's captain, and so on. We have a transmigration of the identity of the shade into the figure of the grave, and when you have the grave, you also have the migration of the place: What was dim, void, or an unnamable place becomes a graveyard. I call this a "figural preparation."

In effect, we can say that every event admits of a figural preparation, that it always possesses a pre-evental *figure*. In our text, the figure is given from the moment that the shades become the ontological symbol of an existence. What is the ontological symbol of an existence, if not the gravestone, on which we find the name, as well as the dates of birth and death, effaced? This is the moment when existence is ready to present itself as its own symbol of being and when being receives its third name: Neither void nor dim, but graveyard.

The grave presents the moment when, by a mutation internal to saying, existence attains a symbolism of being such that the nature of what one will be able to pronounce with regard to being changes drastically. An altered ontological scene doubles the last state, which proves to be not the last, but only the latest. There is a state supernumerary to the last state—precisely the one that constitutes itself all of a sudden. Having been figurally prepared, an event is what happens so that the latest state of being will not be the last.

And what will remain in the end? Well, a saying on a background [*fond*] of nothing or of night: The saying of the "on," of the "nohow on," the imperative of saying as such. Ultimately, this saying is the terminus of a sort of astral language, floating above its own ruin and on the basis of which all can begin again, all can and must recommence. This ineluctable recommencement can be called the unnamable of saying, its "on."[8] And the good—that is, the proper mode of the good within saying—is to sustain the "on." That is all. To sustain it without naming it. To sustain the "on" and to sustain it at the extreme, incandescent point at which its sole apparent content is: "nohow on."

But in order for this to be, an event must go beyond the last state of being. Then, and only then, can I and must I continue. Unless, in order to recreate the conditions for obeying this imperative, one must fall asleep a little—the time needed to conjoin, in a simulacrum of the void, the dim half-light of being and the intoxication of the event. Perhaps the entire difference between Beckett and Mallarmé lies here. The first forbids sleep, as he forbids death. One must remain awake. For the second, after the work of poetry, one can also return to the shade—through the suspension of the question, through the saving interruption. This is because Mallarmé, having posited, once and for all, that a Book is possible, can rest content with "tries in view of better" [*d'essais en vue du mieux*] and sleep between attempts. In this regard, I approve of his being a French faun, rather than an Irish insomniac.

§ 10 Philosophy of the Faun

References

In 1865, Mallarmé is at work on a piece destined for the theater, entitled *Monologue of a Faun*. This text is well and truly conceived for theatrical performance, as attested to by the numerous stage directions it features, detailing both movements and postures. The preparatory sketches organize it into three parts: the afternoon of a faun, the dialogue of the nymphs, and the awakening of the faun. The dramatic construction is at base remarkably simple: The evocation of what has taken place is followed by the presentation of the characters; the awakening, in turn, by the distribution of all the elements of the piece within the dimension of the dream.

This first version begins with the following lines:

> I had nymphs. Is it a dream? No: the clear
> Ruby of their raised breasts still sets the immobile air
> Alight.

Ten years later, in 1875, not having found a taker in the theater, the "monologue"—now under the title of *Improvisation of a Faun*—is set down by Mallarmé in an intermediary version, which begins with:

> These nymphs, I wish to dazzle them.

In 1876, finally, the text with which we are now familiar is published in the form a luxurious booklet featuring a drawing by Manet. The definitive start is the following:

These nymphs, I wish to perpetuate them.

What an exemplary trajectory. The first version aims at a debate over the reality of the object of desire ("I had"), about which a decision is finally reached (it was but a dream). The second version fixes an imperative that could be defined as that of artistic sublimation, whatever the status of its object may be ("to dazzle"). The third version assigns thought a task: Even if the vanishing of what had once emerged has now taken place, the poem must guarantee its perpetual truth.

Architecture: The Hypotheses and the Name

The entire poem stands in the gap between the demonstrative *these*, on the one hand, and the *I* that sustains the imperative of perpetuation, on the other. What relation is there between the genesis of this *I* and the apparent objectivity of *these nymphs*? How can a subject find support in an object when this object has disappeared and the *I* itself remains its only witness? It is through the poem that a disappearance comes to confer its entire being to a subject who takes shelter in a pure act of naming: "these nymphs."

That what is in question falls under this name—*nymphs*—cannot be put in doubt. Naming is the fixed point of the poem, and the faun is at once its product and its guarantor. The poem is nothing but a long fidelity to this name.

What has disappeared under the name can only be supposed. It is these suppositions that, little by little, construct the faun in the gap between the name *these nymphs* and the *I*.

The occupation of this gap is carried out by way of successive hypotheses, connected and worked through by doubt under the fixity of the name.

What are these hypotheses? There are four principal ones, each with its internal ramifications.

1. The nymphs could have been nothing more than imaginary invocations elicited by the force of the faun's desire (they would be "but a yearning of [its] fabulous senses").

2. They could have been mere fictions, aroused this time by the faun's art (he is a musician).

3. These nymphs could indeed be real. The event of their arrival would

then have taken place, but the faun's haste—a kind of premature sexual grasp—would have divided and suppressed the nymphs. This would be the faun's "crime."

4. Perhaps the nymphs are nothing but the fugitive incarnations of a single name: Here, "nymphs" names the hypostases of Venus. The event to which these nymphs testify is immemorial, and the true name, which must arrive, is sacred—it is the name of a goddess.

Constructed through the linkage of these hypotheses, two certainties elucidate the poem and construct the "I" of the faun:

—Whatever else may be the case, the nymphs are no longer there. They are now "these nymphs," and it is without significance, or even dangerous, to wish to remember what they were. Since the event has been abolished, no memory can serve as its guardian. Memory is a de-eventalization, since it attempts to connect the act of naming to a meaning.

—Having left every memory together with every reality behind, from this moment on, the name will become a question of knowing:

Couple, farewell; I shall see the shade that you've become.

The hypotheses suggest that the poem fixes the rule of a fidelity. Fidelity to the name of an event.

Doubts and Traces

We pass from one hypothesis to another by way of methodical doubts. Each doubt sublates the previous hypothesis, and each time there appears the question of what traces the supposed name of the referent would have left within the present situation. The traces themselves must be redecided *as* traces, since none of them counts as an "objective" proof that the event has taken place (that the nymphs have empirically haunted the place):

My breast, virgin of proof, vouches a mysterious
Bite, from some illustrious tooth.

These lines of verse tell us that there are traces, but that these traces do not as such constitute proof, they must be redecided. If one is in the element of fidelity, one will find connections that are sensitive to the name of the event, but none of these will ever amount to proof that what took place did indeed take place.

Doubt, which depends on the name, is the latent vehicle for the fact that what will have taken place, by the time the poem comes to its conclusion, is the truth of desire, as it is captured and fixed by Art, i.e. by the poem itself. We must keep in mind that the poem pins this truth down only under the naming effect of an event that the successive hypotheses, together with the doubts that affect them, demonstrate to be undecidable. This will also be the truth of the inaugural "I," the one who wishes to perpetuate "these nymphs": The "I" is the subject of the undecidable as such.

Of the Prose within the Poem

The poem includes long passages in italics and quotation marks, introduced by capitalized words: RELATE, MEMORIES. An emphatic punctuation is thereby composed, creating a certain intrigue. Opened up by these capitalized imperatives, we find a rather simple narrative style. Under what conditions do these stories intervene, strongly underlined as they are by the italics and quotation marks? The poem speaks clearly: None of these stories (there are three), which invoke the carnal presence of the nymphs, has the least chance of saving the event, whatever this event may be. An event is named, but it can be neither recited nor narrated.

Consequently, the stories have no function besides that of suggesting materials for doubt. They are fragments of memory, to be dissolved. And perhaps this is the function of every story. Let us then define "the story" as that thing about which there is doubt. The story is essentially doubtful—not because it's not true, but because it suggests materials for (poetic) doubt. It's at this point that prose enters the frame. Let us call "prose" every articulation between the story and doubt. The art of prose is neither the art of the story nor the art of doubt, it is the art of proposing the one to the other. This is the case even though prose might be classified on the basis of a predominance of a delight for the story or of an austere presentation of doubt. The first type of prose is the furthest away from the poem. The second is very intimately exposed to it and thus risks coming undone.

The passages in italics and between quotation marks in *The Afternoon of a Faun* are this poem's moments of prose.

The problem is knowing if poetry is always obliged to expose the story prosaically to the doubt of the poem. Hugo's epic style majestically answers: "Yes!" Baudelaire's reply is more nuanced, though it has often been

noted that in *Les fleurs du mal* there is a strong local presence of the prosaic element, an indubitable function of the story. Mallarmé's evolution
between 1865 and his death represents a continuous move away from
Hugo, but also away from Baudelaire. What is at stake is the elimination
of all moments of prose. The core of the poem becomes an enigma, that
of a doubt that must resolve itself into affirmation without having the
story as the material for its exercise. There is no other cause behind what
is often, and mistakenly, referred to as Mallarmé's "hermeticism."

The *Faun* itself is not yet hermetic. Prose figures within it, albeit de-
limited and almost derided by the surfeit of italics and quotation marks.

There are ten moments in the poem, in the sense that one would speak
of ten sections in music.

Section zero, the one that precedes the count, is the first segment of the
first line: "These nymphs, I wish to perpetuate them." We have already
said that this line presents the general program of the poem: To sustain a
subject through fidelity to the name of a vanished and undecidable event.

Let us then examine these ten sections.

1) Dissolution of the Event in its Supposed Place

> So clear,
> Their light carnation, that it turns in the air
> Drowsy with dense slumbers.

Transparency of air and latency of slumber: Just as in the *Coup de dés*
the feather floats over the abyss "without strewing it or fleeing" [*sans le
joncher ni fuir*], the vanished nymphs, reduced to the semblance of a color,
are (perhaps) scattered over the place where the faun does not himself
know if he is waking up or falling asleep.

2) The Putting in Place of Doubt

> Did I love a dream?
> My doubt, hoard of ancient night, ends
> In many a subtle branch, which, since the true woods
> Themselves remain, proves, alas! that all alone I offered myself
> Triumph in the ideal fault of roses—let us
> Reflect . . .

This doubt is not at all of the skeptical type. The imperative is "Re-flect." The entire operation of the poem is an operation of thought—not of remembrance or anamnesis—and doubt is a positive operation of the poem. It is what justifies the inspection of the place as governed by the traces of the nymphs-event. This is the case even though the first inference of doubt is a purely negative one (I was alone, "nothing has taken place but the place").

3) From Desire to Music

> or if the women of your glosses
> Be but a yearning of your fabulous senses!
> Faun, the illusion escapes from the cold, blue
> Eyes, like a weeping spring, of the chastest one:
> But the other all sighs, you say she contrasts
> Like a day breeze warm upon your fleece?
> But no! through the immobile and weary swoon
> Stifling the cool morning with heat if it resists,
> Murmurs no water that my flute does not pour
> On the grove sprinkled with harmonies; and the only wind
> Prompt to exhale from the twin pipes before
> It disperses the sound in an arid rain,
> Is, on the horizon unstirred by a wrinkle,
> The visible and serene artificial breath
> Of inspiration, regaining the sky.

What allows us to pass from the hypothesis of an invention of desire to that of an arousal by art is the "elemental" metamorphosis of the two nymphs. In the undecidability of their emergence, they can be regarded in effect as equivalent to the spring and the breeze, to the water and the air. Art has always been capable of these ancient equations.

This section intertwines two things that will not be separated again. These are, on the one hand, a procedure placed on the side of desire and love, and, on the other, the artistic procedure. The latter is itself endowed with a twofold status: Depicted *within* the poem by the musical art of the faun, it is also the becoming of the poem itself. Basically, there are here three intersecting registers: desire, tied to the supposed encounter with the nudity of the nymphs; the art of the (musician) faun, creator of elemental fictions; the art of the poet. The erotic summoning supports an intrapo-

etic metaphor of the poem, which is superimposed, by means of metamorphoses and chains of equivalence, onto the inferred play of desire:
nymphs → cold blue eyes → tears → spring → murmur of the flute → capacity of the poem.

4) Extorting from the Place the Name of the Event

> O Sicilian edges of a tranquil marsh
> That, rivaling the suns, my vanity plunders,
> Silent beneath the flowering sparks, RELATE
> *"How I was cutting here the hollow reeds*
> *That talent tamed; when, on the glaucous gold*
> *Of distant verdures vowing their vines to the fountains*
> *An animal whiteness languorously sways:*
> *And to the slow prelude whence the pipes are born,*
> *This flight of swans—no! of Naiads—flees*
> *Or dives . . . "*

In these lines we have an example, which is still very simple, of what is
without doubt the most general movement of Mallarmé's poems: The presentation of the place, followed by the attempt to discern within it the
proof of some vanished event.

The above passage includes a first sequence of the story in italics and
between quotation marks. This story—attributed to the place itself, as if
it was about to confess the event that haunts it—is a pure moment of
prose that already persuades us that it will result only in doubt. Moreover,
this result is inscribed into the interrogative oscillation between "swans"
and "Naiads," leaving open the possibility of a subversion of reality (the
birds of the marsh) by the imaginary (the nudity of the women). Finally,
the story can indeed lead us back to the solitude of the place, thereby exposing the faun to his first temptation.

5) The First Temptation: To Abolish Oneself
Ecstatically within the Place

> Inert, all burns in the tawny hour
> Without marking the art whereby this desired excess
> Hymen fled entire from he who seeks the *A*:

> Then I will awaken to the primal fervor,
> Upright and alone, under an ancient wave of light,
> O lilies! and one among you all in artlessness.

Since the narration of the place cannot persuade, proposing as it does only a vain memory, why not give up searching for traces? Why not allow oneself to be simply consumed by the light of the landscape? This is the temptation of infidelity, that of abdicating on the questions of the event and of the fidelity to the name, the fidelity to "nymphs." Since a truth is always induced by some event (otherwise, where would its power of novelty come from?), every temptation against truth presents itself as a temptation to renounce the event and its naming, to be content with the pure "there is," with the definitive force of the place alone. Consumed by the light of noon, the faun would be unburdened of his problem; he would be "one among us" and no longer this subjective singularity delivered over to the undecidable. Every ecstasy of the place is the abandonment of a tiring truth. But this is only a temptation. The desire of the faun, his music and, finally, the poem persist in the search for signs.

6) The Signs of the Body and the Power of Art

> Besides this sweet nothing by their lip disclosed,
> The kiss, which hushed assures the faithless,
> My breast, virgin of proof, vouches a mysterious
> Bite, from some illustrious tooth;
> But enough! such arcanum chose as confidant
> The vast twin reed played beneath the azure:
> Which, diverting to itself the cheeks' turmoil,
> Dreams, in a long solo, that we may divert
> The environing beauty by false confusions
> Between itself and our credulous song;
> And, as high as love can modulate, to efface
> From the banal dream of pure backs
> Or flanks tracked with my gazes shut,
> A sonorous, vain, monotonous line.

In the first two lines of this section, the faun states that there is another trace than the kiss, or the memory of a kiss. The kiss "in itself" is pure nullification, a "sweet nothing." But there is the trace, a mysterious bite.

One will obviously remark the apparent contradiction between "virgin of proof" and "vouches . . . a bite" in the same line. This contradiction constitutes a thesis: No attested trace of an event amounts to proof of its having taken place. The event is subtracted from proof, otherwise, it would lose its dimension of undecidable vanishing. Yet it is not ruled out that there is a trace or sign, even if, since it is not an element of proof, this sign does not constrain its own interpretation. An event can very well leave traces, but these traces never have a univocal value in themselves. In fact, it is impossible to interrogate the traces of an event except under the hypothesis of an act of naming. Traces can signify an event only if this event has been decided. Under the fixed and long-decided name of "nymphs," without producing proof, you can vouch a "mysterious" bite.

That is the very essence of the Mallarméan notion of mystery: A trace that does not amount to proof, a sign whose referent is not imposed upon us. There is mystery every time that something signals without one thereby being constrained to an interpretation. The sign is the sign of the undecidable itself under the fixity of the name.

Beginning with the "But" of line 43 ("But enough!"), Mallarmé develops the hypothesis that this mysterious trace is itself really a production of art. If we compare this to the first version, we can see that the arrangement is very different. In the first version, the mysterious bite was called "feminine," so that its interpretation was fixed. No mystery in literature here. Between 1865 and 1876, Mallarmé moves from the idea of a univocal proof to that of a mysterious trace, a trace whose interpretation remains open. This is because the first version partakes in the register of knowledge. The question that motivates the poem, even in its theatrical destination, is the following: What do we know about what has taken place? Proof (the feminine bite) and knowledge are linked together. In the last version, the testimony becomes a sign whose referent is suspended. The question is no longer that of knowing what has taken place, but rather that of making truth out of an undecidable event. Mallarmé replaces the old romantic question of dream and reality with that of the evental origin of the true and of its relation to the givenness of a place. These are the components of the mystery.

The poem says: My artist's flute has chosen, as its proper confidant, as the one it trusts, precisely such a mystery. "Mystery" functions from then on as the respondent of the flute's musical "I," opening the way for a renewal of the hypothesis according to which the referent of the mystery is artistic, rather than amorous.

The very intricate lines from 46 to 48 (beginning with "Which, diverting to itself . . . ") state that the flute, leading what could testify for desire and turmoil back to itself, establishes a musical reverie for the sake of art alone. The artist and his art diverted the décor by establishing ambivalences between the beauty of the place, on the one hand, and their credulous song, on the other. The flute that the artist plays beneath the sky was able to take such a mystery as its confidant by leading all the virtualities of desire back to itself. The flute diverts the entire beauty of the place by establishing a constant ambivalence with the artist's song. With the same intensity that love is capable of, it dreams of causing to vanish or dissolve the fantasmatic dream that one may have of some body or other.[1] The flute has the power of drawing from this material of the dream "A sonorous, vain, monotonous line."

The evident affectation of this passage, its indulgent preciousness, underlines the fact that the mystery of the dream that has vanished from the desired bodies may simply be an effect of art and does not require us to suppose the existence of an event. If it is registered by art, a desire without encounter, without a real object, can arouse a mysterious trace within the situation (which is capable of establishing "confusions").

The artistic trace is mysterious because it is a trace only of itself.

Mallarmé's idea is that art is capable of producing a trace in the world, which, since it relates only to the tracing, remains closed upon its own enigma. Art can create the trace of a desire devoid of an encountered object (in the sense of a real object). That is its mystery—the mystery of its equivalence to desire, without recourse to any object.

That is what exposes us to the second temptation.

7) Second Temptation: To Be Content with the Artistic Simulacrum

> Try then, instrument of flights, O Syrinx malign
> To bloom again by the lakes where you await me!
> Of my clamor proud, long will I speak
> Of goddesses; and by idolatrous paintings
> Strip more cinctures from their shade:
> So, when I've sucked the brightness out of grapes,
> To banish a regret that my pretense discarded,
> Laughing, I raise the empty cluster to the summer sky

And, blowing into its luminous skins, craving
Drunkenness, until evening I gaze through.

Since the previous hypothesis is that everything derives from art, the transition is addressed to the faun's flute. The poem says: "You, instrument of art, go and recommence your task"; "I wish to return to my desire, of which you pretend to be the equal."

The desiring faun is here distinguished from the artistic faun. At the same time, however, the erotic scene is presented as pure reverie, and consequently the event (the real advent of the nymphs) is nullified. We are here in the midst of the second temptation, which is that of being content, subjectively, with the simulacrum, with an objectless desire. This could be referred to as a perverse interpretation of the previous hypothesis. It amounts to saying: "Perhaps it is really my art that created this mystery, but I will fill it with a desiring simulacrum. Here I will find my enjoyment." It then becomes essential that the simulacrum thus conceived be an intoxication, an intoxication that diverts us from all truth. If the simulacrum is possible, then I no longer have any need for fidelity, since I can imitate or render artificial what has made itself absent, treating it qua void, which is also a void of sensation (the grapes filled with air). A simulacrum is always the replacement of a fidelity to the event by the staging of a void.

In the question of the event, the function of the void is central, because what the event summons, what it causes to arise, is the void of a situation. By making the Real fall on the side of "what was not there," the event testifies that the being of the "there is" is the void. The event undoes the appearance of the full. An event is the injection of lack into an instance of plenitude.

But since the event vanishes, and only its name subsists, there is no other veridical way to treat this void in the reconstituted situation than by being faithful to the additional name (in this case, by being faithful to the nymphs). However, there still lingers a nostalgia for the void itself, such as it had been summoned up in the flash of the event. This is the tempting nostalgia of a full void, an inhabitable void, a perpetual ecstasy. Of course, this nostalgia demands the blindness of intoxication.

This is what the faun abandons himself to and against which he finds no other resort than the brutal resumption of narrative memory.

8) The Scene of the Crime

O nymphs, let us swell with divers MEMORIES.
"Piercing the reeds, my eye speared each immortal
Neck, that drowns its burning in the wave
With a cry of rage flung to the forest sky;
And the splendid wash of tresses disappears
In radiances and shudders, O jewels!
I hasten; when, at my feet, entwine (bruised
By the languor tasted in this harm of being two)
Girls asleep in nothing but each other's perilous arms;
I seize them, not untangling, and fly up
To these heights, hated by the frivolous shade,
Of roses draining all their scent from the sun,
Where our frolics should be like the day, spent."
I adore you, ire of virgins, O fierce delight
Of the sacred naked burden that slips to flee
My fire-drinking lip, like lightning
Shudders! the secret fright of the flesh:
From the feet of the inhuman to the heart of the shy
Abandoned at once by an innocence, moist
With mad tears or vapors less sad.
"My crime, gay at vanquishing these traitorous
Fears, is to have parted the disheveled tuft
Of kisses that the gods had so well raveled;
For, as I was about to hide an ardent laugh
In the happy folds of one alone (holding
By a simple finger—so that her feathery candor
Should be stained by the ardor of her burning
Sister, the little one, naïve, and unblushing:)
When from my arms, loosened by vague deaths,
This prey, ungrateful to the end, frees itself
With no pity for the sob that still intoxicated me."

This long sequence vigorously depends on the internal prose, on the italics of the story and the vain pretence of memory. Without detours or distractions, it tells us first of how the faun seized the pair of nymphs and then of how he lost them, the two beauties vanishing in his embrace. The eroticism here is insistent, almost vulgar ("moist with . . . vapors less sad," "the ardor of her burning sister," etc.). This is not the "vague literature" of Verlaine (an obscene poet himself, as is well known) or the "allusive, never direct" words of Mallarmé himself (an equally obscene poet, see *Une négresse par le démon secouée* [A negress possessed by the devil]).

The first story, in the fourth section, belonged to the regime of the summoning of the place. The "Sicilian borders of a tranquil marsh" were meant to confess the nymphs-event that had affected them. The two stories in this eighth section are directly entrusted to memory ("we swell with divers MEMORIES"). Is there a narrative coincidence? Not entirely. The first prosaic occurrence tells only of the disappearance of the nymphs. It is centered on the vanishing dimension of the event. This time, instead, we have a positive description in the form of an erotic scene that identifies the name ("these nymphs") and ratifies its plurality (the two women are clearly distinguished, at the same time as their relative indistinction is affirmed, since the gods keep them "raveled").

But what use is the erotic precision of these memories for the becoming true of the poem?

Memory is marked by this essential ambivalence, which is that it is under the sign of the name. The place may very well be innocent of the event. Memory itself never is, since it is prestructured by naming. Memory claims to bring us the event as such, but this is an imposture, because its entire narration is dominated by the imperative of the name and could end up being nothing but a (logical and retroactive) exercise elicited by the unshakeable assertion "these nymphs."

There is never any memory of the pure event. Its aspect of abolition means that it is never mnemonic. It is the innocence of the place and the ambivalence of traces that prevail on this point. There is memory only of what can be elicited by the fixity of the name. This is why, as precise as it may be, it turns out that this sequence proposes nothing but new materials for doubt.

The first of the two stories in the sequence evokes the sleepy entanglement of the two nymphs and their seizure by the faun's desire. The second evokes the disappearance, by forced division, of this bicephalous nude.

The fantasmatic lesbian kernel of the story is patent. Poetically inaugurated by Baudelaire, it runs through the whole century, painting included (just think of Courbet's sleepers). In this common motif, we can doubtless expect some underlying meditation on the One and the Two ("this harm of being two"). This is because everything depends on maintaining the entanglement of the same to the same.

There are two essential moments in this meditation, line 72 ("I seize them, not untangling") and lines 83 and 84 ("My crime, gay at vanquishing these traitorous / Fears, is to have parted the disheveled tuft"). Entanglement and disentanglement; the One of the Two and the fatal Two of the One.

The two tangled women constitute a self-sufficient totality, the fantasy of a desire closed upon itself, devoted to itself, a desire without an other—or should we say a noncastrated desire? In any case, a desire of the Two *as One*. It is this circular or looped desire that arouses the external desire of the faun and that will also lead him into perdition. What the faun fails to understand is that the encounter of the nymphs is not an encounter *for* his desire, but an encounter *of* desire. The faun treats as an object (and therefore tries to divide, to treat "partially") what could exist only as a totality precisely by doing without any object, by presenting the figure of pure desire.

The painful lesson imparted on the faun is the following: When it comes to a veritable event, it is never a question of an object of desire, but of desire as such, pure desire. The lesbian allegory is the closed presentation of this purity.

One will pay particular heed to the passage (lines 76 to 82, interruption of the italics) that separates the two stories in this section. We are dealing here with the only properly subjectivized moment ("I adore you, ire of virgins"), the moment when desire is *declared*.

It is important to distinguish declaration from naming. The naming ("these nymphs") having already taken place, let us call "declaration" the fact of stating one's own relation to this naming. This is the crucial moment of the induction of the subject under the name of the event. Every subject declares itself ("I adore you") as a relation to naming. Consequently, the declaration is also that of the subject's desiring fidelity to the event.

The declaration of the faun is interpolated between two moments of the story, the first of which is under the sign of the One and the second under the sign of division. The faun makes this declaration as he confesses not having known how to remain faithful to the One of pure desire.

There is infidelity every time that the declaration proves itself heterogeneous to the naming or is inscribed in a subjective series other than the one imposed by naming. That is exactly the faun's "crime."

This crime is to have attempted, under the sign of a heterogeneous desiring declaration (wanting to unite erotically with the two nymphs, taken separately), the disjunction of that whose Oneness, as a pure desire absorbing the Two, was guarded by the gods, conceived as the indivisible power of evental emergence. The crime is to make an object of what arises wholly otherwise than an object. The subjectivizing force of an event is not the desire for an object, but the desire of a desire.

This is what Mallarmé tells us: Whoever restores the category of the object, which the event always revokes, is led back to abolition, pure and simple. The nymphs dissolve in the arms of the one who wished to turn them into the object of his own desire instead of being consequent with the encounter of a new desire. The only trace of the event left for him will be the feeling of a loss.

When the event comes to be, objectivation (the "crime") summons loss. This is the great problem of the fidelity to an event, of the ethics of fidelity: How not to restore the object and objectivity?

Objectivation is analysis, as well as the narrative vice of memory. The faun analyzes a memory and is lost in objectivity.

The faun, or at least the faun of memory, the prosaic faun, was not able capable of being what the event demands us to be: An objectless subject.

9) Third Temptation: The Single and Sacred Name

> Too bad! others will lead me toward happiness,
> Their tresses knotted to the horns upon my brow;
> You, my passion, know, that crimson and already ripe,
> Each pomegranate bursts, murmuring with bees;
> And our blood, taken with the one who will seize it,
> Flows for the whole eternal swarm of desire.
> When these woods are awash with gold and ashes
> At that hour a feast exults among the spent leafage:
> Etna! it is among you by Venus visited
> Setting her artless heels upon your lava
> As a sad slumber thunders or the flame expires.
> I hold the queen!
>
>   O sure punishment . . .
>   No,

Forever unfaithful, at first the faun adopts the classical position of the one who renounces being the subject of an event: Nothing unique has happened, six of one, half a dozen of the other, and so on. The dissolution of singularity in repetition. This is, of course, to subtract oneself from naming, as indicated by the fact that "others" can come to occupy the place of "these nymphs." This repetitious alterity, which no longer harbors anything but the monotony of abstract desire, is the traditional veil that covers the abandonment of all truth. For all that, a truth could never be indicated by the "Too bad!" of the strong spirit, any more than by the "so much the better" of the troubled one.

Yet under this camouflaged position, which is governed by the feeling of loss, another stance ripens, a prophetic stance, the announcement of the return of what was lost. This is surely a more interesting figure. About an event only the disappearance of which is now subjectivized, one can prophesy its return, and even its (eternal) Return, since the force of desire, in its link to loss, is always there. The availability of nameless, anonymous desire nourishes the announcement of the return. This is because it is for "the whole eternal swarm of desire" that the singular encounter has not taken place, the principle of which can therefore return.

The difficulty that perpetuates the crime is that this return is inevitably that of an object. And even, as we shall see, of the hypostasis of object into the Object: The Thing or the God.

This section confirms that little faith should be accorded to memory, since all it does is unfold the crime all the way to its transcendent consequences. Under the falsely joyful sign of the "Too bad!" there subsists the analytic and objective disposition. All of a sudden, it is the loss that will return, which is essentially the loss of "these nymphs."

Inversely, what one can be faithful to is characterized by its not repeating. A truth is in the element of the unrepeatable. The repetition of the object or the loss (it's the same thing) is nothing but a deceptive infidelity to the unrepeatable singularity of the true.

The faun will try to occlude this deception in advance by invoking the absolute object. No longer women, but Woman, no longer loves, but the goddess of love, no longer courtesans [*sujettes*], but the queen. Woven from the image of the swarm, which is itself articulated upon abstract desire, Venus descends upon the place as the inexistent queen of the bees of the Real.

The third temptation thus enters the stage, the temptation of a naming by a single and sacred name, such that the idea of the encounter's singularity is abandoned in favor of a definite and immemorial name.

This advent of the sacred name is carefully and theatrically staged. We witness a change of lighting and décor. We enter into the twilight of the poem. The solar marsh is replaced with the motif of the volcano and lava ("When these woods are awash with gold and ashes"). The logic of the "too bad" prepares the prenocturnal atmosphere of deception ("as a sad slumber thunders or the flame expires"). This is a good image of the conditions for the emergence of a factitious transcendence: It is of the essence of god always to arrive too late. The god is never anything but the last temptation.

The abrupt "sure punishment" indicates a lucid and motiveless leap on the part of the faun (and the poet): The temptation of the sacred, of the single name to which the naming of the event is to be sacrificed, of the Venus, that takes the place of every singular nymph, of the Object that nullifies every Real—all this would lead to extremely grave consequences (to wit, the collapse of the poem into some sort of romantic prophesy). The temptation is revoked.

10) The Conclusive Meaning of Sleep and Shadow

> but the soul
> Of words vacant and this body grown heavier
> To noon's proud silence at last succumb:
> At once we must sleep in the forgetfulness of blasphemy
> Stretched upon the thirsty sand, and how I love to open
> My mouth to the stellar efficacy of wines!
>
> Couple, farewell; I shall see the shade that you've become.

Casting doubt upon the crepuscular and ashen figure of the goddess, the faun is restored to the noon of his truth. It is this suspended truth that the faun will rejoin in his sleep.

It is important to connect this sleep, this second intoxication—which is very distant from the one that accompanied the musical simulacrum—to the terminal motif of the shadow, of the inspection of what it will have become. The shadow of the couple is what the name "these nymphs" will have forever induced in the poem. The faun tells us: Under the protection of the name, I will go and see what "these nymphs" (the invariable name) will have been. The shadow is the Idea in the future perfect of its poetic procession.

The shadow is the truth of the encounter with the nymphs that the faun aims to perpetuate. Doubt is what has permitted the faun to resist the successive temptations. Sleep is this tenacious immobility in which the faun can linger, having passed from the name to the truth of the name (a movement that makes up the poem in its entirety) and from "faun" to the anonymous "I" whose whole being lies in having perpetuated the nymphs.

Sleep is compact fidelity, tenacity, and continuity. This last fidelity is the very act of the subject as it has now become. It is "of words vacant" because it no longer needs to experiment with hypotheses. And it possesses a "body grown heavier" because it no longer has any need for the agitation of desire.

Unlike Lacan's subject, which is desire concocted by words, the Mallarméan subject of poetic truth is neither soul nor body, neither language nor desire. It is both act and place, an anonymous obstinacy that finds its metaphor in sleep.

Simply put, "I shall see" the place whence originates the possibility of poem in its entirety. "I" will write this poem. This seeing of sleep will begin with "These nymphs, I want to perpetuate them."

Between "these nymphs" and the "I" of their perpetuation, between the evental disappearance of the naked beauties and the anonymity of the slumbering faun, there will have been the fidelity of the poem. It alone subsists forever.

Summary

I) THE EVENT

The poem reminds us of its undecidability. This is one of Mallarmé's greatest motifs. Nothing within a situation—salon, tomb, marsh, or surface of the sea—can force the recognition of the event *as* event. The question of the chance of the event, of the undecidability of its belonging, is such that, as numerous as its traces may be, the event remains dependent on its declaration.

The event has two faces. Thought in its being, it is an anonymous supplement, an uncertainty, a fluctuation of desire. We cannot really describe the advent of the nymphs. Thought according to its name, the event is an imperative of fidelity. These nymphs will have been, but it is only by plotting out the poem's obedience to this injunction that the truth of this having taken place is produced.

2) THE NAME

It is fixed. "These nymphs"—that will not change, regardless of the doubts and the temptations. This invariability belongs to the new situation, that of the awakening faun. The name is the present—the only present—of the event. The question of truth can be formulated as follows: What is to be done with a nominal present? The poem exhausts all the options, and concludes that around the name a truth is created that will have been the traversing of these options—including the worst ones, the temptations of doing nothing with the gift of the present.

3) FIDELITY

a) Negatively, the poem outlines a complete theory of infidelity. Its most immediate form is memory, that is, narrative or historical infidelity. Being faithful to an event never entails remembering. On the contrary, it always refers to the uses one makes of the name of an event. But beyond the peril of memory, the poem exhibits three figures of temptation, three ways of capitulating:
—The identification with the place, or the figure of ecstasy. Abandoning the supernumerary name, this figure abolishes the subject into the permanence of the place.
—The choice of the simulacrum. Accepting the fictitious character of the name, this figure fills its void with a desiring plenitude. The subject is then nothing other than intoxicated omnipotence in which the void and the full become indistinguishable.
—The choice of a single immemorial name that overhangs and crushes the singularity of the event.
We could say that ecstasy, plenitude, and the sacred are the three temptations that, from within an evental emergence, organize its corruption and denial.
b) Positively, the poem establishes the existence of an operator of fidelity, which in this instance is to be located in the pair formed by the hypotheses and the doubt that assails them. An aleatory trajectory is com-

posed on this basis that explores the entire situation in terms of the fixed name, experimenting and overcoming the temptations and concluding with the future perfect of the subject that this trajectory has become. The types of trajectories taken into account here—in terms of the determination of the "I" in the grip of the name "these nymphs"—fall under the registers of amorous desire and poetic production.

On the desire that attaches itself to the name of what disappeared depends the possibility that, once this desire is revoked, a subject can be woven from the singular truth that it unknowingly allowed to become.

Source Materials

Published texts used as materials in the composition of this book:

"Art et philosophie," in *Artistes et philosophes: Éducateurs?*, ed. Christian Descamps (Paris: Centre Georges-Pompidou, 1994).

"Philosophie et poésie au point de l'innomable," in *Po&sie* 64 (1993).

"La danse comme métaphore de la pensée," in *Danse et Pensée*, ed. Ciro Bruni (Paris: GERMS, 1993).

"Dix thèses sur le théâtre," in *Les Cahiers de le Comédie-Française* (Paris, 1995).

"Le cinema comme faux mouvement," in *L'Art du cinéma* 4 (1994).

"Peut-on parler d'un film?," in *L'Art du cinéma* 6 (1994).

Translator's Notes

Translator's Note

1. See Stéphane Mallarmé, *Selected Poems*, trans. C. F. MacIntyre (Berkeley: University of California Press, 1957), pp. 46–55, and Stéphane Mallarmé, *Collected Poems*, trans. Henry Weinfield (Berkeley: University of California Press, 1994), pp. 38–41.

2. See Alain Badiou, "La méthode de Mallarmé: Soustraction et isolement," in *Conditions* (Paris: Seuil, 1991), pp. 109–10. On the issue of Badiou and translation, see Charles Ramond's insightful essay "Système et traduction chez Alain Badiou," in *Alain Badiou: Penser le multiple*, ed. Charles Ramond (Paris: L'Harmattan, 2002), pp. 525–40.

Chapter 1

1. Badiou is here alluding to the critique of Heideggerian poetics that served as the focus of a seminar at the Collège International de Philosophie and that was later the object of a volume edited by Jacques Rancière, *La politique des poètes* (Paris: Albin Michel, 1992), to which Badiou himself contributed the essay "L'âge des poètes" (pp. 21–38). The subtitle of this volume was *Pourquoi des poètes en temps de détresse*. Heidegger's notion of "distress" [*Not*] appears prominently in his *Contributions to Philosophy (From Enowning)*, trans. Parvis Emad and Kenneth Maly (Bloomington: Indiana University Press, 1999), section 17.

2. In using the expression *prend barre*, Badiou is alluding to the Lacanian theory of the four discourses, and in particular to Lacan's schema for the discourse of the hysteric. In this discourse, the subject (denoted in Lacan by a barred S) "takes charge" [*prend barre*] of the master signifier (S1), in such a way that it leads knowledge (S2) to produce the *objet petit a* as the truth of the hysteric, which is

in turn represented in Lacan's diagram by an *a* lying beneath the bar that separates it from the barred S. Badiou's allusion is thus to the two senses of the bar, the bar *within* the hysteric subject and the one *over* the *objet petit a*, which the hysteric (in the position of the "agent") attains as her own truth by displacing the master to the dominated position (or position of the "other"). See Jacques Lacan, *On Feminine Sexuality, the Limits of Love and Knowledge (Seminar XX)*, ed. Jacques-Alain Miller, trans. Bruce Fink (New York: Norton, 1998), pp. 16–17. For a lucid explanation of this aspect of Lacanian doctrine, see the entry "Discourse" in Dylan Evans, *An Introductory Dictionary of Lacanian Psychoanalysis* (London: Routledge, 1996), pp. 44–46.

3. *Donner du bâton*, literally "giving stick," an expression related to the earlier *prendre barre*, since a *bâton* is also a vertical line.

4. On this Lacanian neologism, see Evans, *An Introductory Dictionary*, pp. 58–59.

5. See Meditation 31 in Alain Badiou, *L'être et l'événement* (Paris: Seuil, 1988), pp. 361–77.

Chapter 2

1. Plato, *Republic* (595a), trans.Paul Shorey, in *The Collected Dialogues of Plato*, ed. Edith Hamilton and Huntington Cairns (Princeton: Princeton University Press, 1989), p. 819. Translation modified.

2. Ibid., (607b), p. 832.

3. Ibid., (608b), p. 833.

4. Plato, *Protagoras* (339a), trans. W. K. C. Guthrie, in *The Collected Dialogues*, p. 339.

5. From "A Throw of the Dice / *Un coup de dés*," in Stéphane Mallarmé, *Collected Poems*, translated and with a commentary by Henry Weinfield (Berkeley: University of California, 1994), pp. 124–25. Translation modified.

6. Stéphane Mallarmé, "Prose (for des Esseintes) / *Prose (pour des Esseintes)*." My translation. A version of this poem can be found in *Collected Poems*, trans. Henry Weinfield (Berkeley: University of California Press, 1994), pp. 46–48.

7. See Alain Badiou, "La méthode de Mallarmé: Soustraction et isolement" and "La méthode de Rimbaud: L'interruption," in *Conditions* (Paris: Éditions du Seuil, 1991), pp. 108–29 and 130–54; see also "Est-il exact que toute pensée émet un coup de dés?," *Les Conférences du Perroquet* 5 (1986): 1–20.

8. Stéphane Mallarmé, *L'Après-midi d'un faune*, in *Collected Poems*, p. 38. Translation modified.

9. The theme of the "there is" [*il y a*] as pure presentation (and *not* presence) accessed and configured by the operations of art recurs throughout the *Handbook*, especially in the treatment of Beckett's *Worstward Ho* in Chapter 9. Its speculative elaboration can be found in Badiou's elucidation of the groundwork

of his ontology in Meditation 1 of his *L'Etre et l'événement* (Paris: Seuil, 1988), pp. 31–39.

10. Arthur Rimbaud, "L'Éternité," in *Poésies / Une saison en enfer / Illuminations* (Paris: Gallimard, 1984), p. 108. All Rimbaud translations are my own.

11. Stéphane Mallarmé, "Hommage / *Homage*," *Collected Poems*, p. 76. Translation modified.

12. Stéphane Mallarmé, "Salutation / *Salut*," *Collected Poems*, p. 3. Translation modified.

13. Stéphane Mallarmé, "Several Sonnets (I) / *Plusieurs sonnets (I)*," *Collected Poems*, p. 66.

14. Arthur Rimbaud, "Matinée d'ivresse," *Poésies*, p. 167.

15. Arthur Rimbaud, "Vagabonds," *Poésies*, p. 174.

16. Stéphane Mallarmé, "Prose (for des Esseintes) / *Prose (pour des Esseintes)*," *Collected Poems*, p. 46. Translation modified.

17. Stéphane Mallarmé, "Sur l'évolution littéraire (enquête de Jules Huret)," in *Igitur, Divagations, Un coup de dés* (Paris: Gallimard, 1976), pp. 391–92.

18. Stéphane Mallarmé, "A Throw of the Dice / *Un coup de dés*," *Collected Poems*, pp. 138–39.

19. Stéphane Mallarmé, "Mystery in Literature / *Le Mystère dans les lettres*," in *Mallarmé in Prose*, ed. Mary Ann Caws (New York: New Directions, 2001), pp. 49–50. Translation modified.

20. Stéphane Mallarmé, "Several Sonnets (IV) / *Plusieurs sonnets (IV)*, *Collected Poems*, p. 69.

21. Arthur Rimbaud, "Alchimie du verbe," *Poésies*, pp. 140, 141.

22. Arthur Rimbaud, "Lettre à George Izambart," *Poésies*, p. 200.

23. Arthur Rimbaud, "Lettre à Paul Demeny," *Poésies*, p. 202.

Chapter 3

1. Stéphane Mallarmé, "Magie," in *Igitur, Divagations, Un coup de dés* (Paris: Gallimard, 1976), p. 304. My translation.

2. Stéphane Mallarmé, "Fragments et Notes," in *Igitur, Divagations, Un coup de dés*, p. 382. My translation.

3. The reference here is to the Lacanian notion of the *passe*. See Evans, *An Introductory Dictionary*, pp. 135–36.

4. Stéphane Mallarmé, "Crise de vers," in *Igitur, Divagations, Un coup de dés*, p. 248. My translation.

5. Stéphane Mallarmé, "Mystery in Literature / *Les mystères dans les lettres*," in *Mallarmé in Prose*, ed. Mary Ann Caws (New York: New Directions, 2001), p. 49.

6. Stéphane Mallarmé, "L'action restreinte," in *Igitur, Divagations, Un coup de dés*, p. 258. My translation.

7. Stéphane Mallarmé, "Mystery in Literature / *Le Mystère dans les lettres*," in *Mallarmé in Prose*, p. 48.

8. Mallarmé, "L'action restreinte," p. 257.

9. Ibid., p. 255.

10. Paul Celan, "Es kommt," from the posthumously published collection *Zeitgehöft: Spät Gedichte aus dem Nachlass* (Frankfurt am Main: Suhrkamp, 1976). New translation by John Felstiner.

11. Paul Celan, "I have cut bamboo" (Ich habe Bambus geschnitten), in the collection *Die Niemandrose* (1963). Translation by John Felstiner. *Selected Poems and Prose of Paul Celan* (New York: Norton, 2001), p. 185.

12. Paul Celan, "An die Haltlosigkeiten," from *Zeitgehöft*. New translation by John Felstiner. Martine Broda, whose French translation is used here by Badiou, renders the first two lines as "Sur les inconsistances / s'appuyer:"—literally, "lean (or support) yourself on inconsistencies." Also, where Felstiner's translation gives "rushes up" the French opts for *se met à bruire*, for a "rustling" that plays into Badiou's thematization of the "murmur of the indiscernible."

13. Stéphane Mallarmé, "Displays / *Étalages*," in *Mallarmé in Prose*, p. 29.

Chapter 4

1. "Vection" is defined in mathematics as a symbol of quantity having magnitude and direction, and in physiology as a strong sensation of self-motion.

Chapter 5

1. Stéphane Mallarmé, "A Throw of the Dice / *Un coup de dés*," in *Collected Poems*, trans. Henry Weinfield (Berkeley: University of California, 1994), pp. 142–43. Translation modified.

2. Labîd ben Rabi'a, "Le Désert et son code," in *Du Désert d'Arabie aux jardins d'Espagne: Chefs-d'œuvre de la poésie arabe classique*, ed. and trans. André Miquel (Arles: Sindbad, 1992). All translations from Labîd ben Rabi'a are my own from the French version.

3. Mallarmé, *Collected Poems*, pp. 130–31.

4. Ibid., pp. 142–43, 130–31.

5. Ibid., pp. 144–45.

6. Ibid., pp. 128–29.

Chapter 6

1. Friedrich Nietzsche, *Thus Spoke Zarathustra*, trans. R. J. Hollingdale (London: Penguin, 1969), p. 210.

2. Ibid., p. 210.

3. Ibid., p. 55.

4. Ibid., p. 129.

5. Ibid., p. 241.

6. Friedrich Nietzsche, *The Case of Wagner*, trans. Walter Kaufmann (New York: Vintage, 1967), p. 180.

7. Stéphane Mallarmé, "Ballets" and "Another Dance Study," in *Mallarmé in Prose*, ed. Mary Ann Caws (New York: New Directions, 2001), pp. 108–16.

8. Stéphane Mallarmé, "Le genre ou des modernes," in *Igitur, Divagations, Coup de dés*, (Paris: Gallimard, 1976), p. 208. My translation.

9. Alain Badiou, *L'Etre et l'événement*, (Paris: Seuil, 1988), pp. 193–98.

10. Stéphane Mallarmé, *Mallarmé in Prose*, p. 115.

11. Ibid., p. 109.

12. Ibid., p. 111.

13. Ibid., p. 109.

14. Ibid.

15. Ibid.

16. Ibid., p. 113. Translation modified.

17. Ibid., p. 112. Translation modified.

Chapter 7

1. "Un théâtre élitaire pour tous" was Antoine Vitez's programmatic slogan for the Théâtre de Chaillot.

Chapter 9

1. All page references in this essay are to *Worstward Ho*, in Samuel Beckett, *Nohow On* (New York: Grove Press, 1996).

2. There are a few exceptions to this general rule, mostly involving brief texts or collaborations: *Molloy* was translated in part in collaboration with Patrick Bowles, *The Expelled* and *The End* were translated in collaboration with Richard Seaver, and the two brief texts *The Image* and *The Cliff* were translated by Édith Fournier.

3. The French *Watt* and *D'un ouvrage abandonné* (From an Abandoned Work) were translated in collaboration with Ludovic and Agnès Janvier; *All That Fall*

(Tous ceux qui tombent) was translated into French by Robert Pinget, and *Embers* (Cendres) by Pinget and Beckett.

4. The theory of the "count as one" [*compte-pour-un*] is expounded by Badiou in Meditation 1 of *L'être et l'événement* (Paris: Éditions du Seuil, 1988), pp. 31–39. The term originates in Jacques-Alain Miller's "La suture: Élements de la logique du signifiant," originally in *Cahiers pour l'analyse* 1 (1966), now reprinted in *Un début dans la vie* (Paris: Gallimard, 2002). Miller's piece is discussed by Badiou in *Le nombre et les nombres* (Paris: Seuil, 1990), pp. 36–44.

5. Badiou is currently developing a systematic approach to the relation between being and appearance, to be presented in his *Logiques des mondes* (Paris: Seuil, 2005). Many of the themes anticipated in these writings on Beckett find their logical and mathematical formalization in this work, sections of which have appeared in English in Alain Badiou, *Theoretical Writings*, ed, and trans. Ray Brassier and Alberto Toscano (London: Continuum, 2004), pp. 189–231.

6. Beckett uses two English terms—"missaid" and "ill said"—where the French, both in Fournier's translation of *Worstward Ho* and Beckett's own of *Ill Seen Ill Said*, has only one: *mal dire* (or *mal dit*). To maintain the juxtaposition with the "well said," as well as Badiou's constant references to *Ill Seen Ill Said*, I have chosen to translate most occurrences of *mal dit* by "ill said" rather than "missaid."

7. Stéphane Mallarmé, "A Throw of the Dice / *Un coup de dés*," in *Collected Poems*, trans. Henry Weinfield (Berkeley: University of California Press, 1994), p. 144.

8. On the unnamable as a concept defining the ethic of truths, see Alain Badiou, "Truth: Facing the Unnameable," in *Theoretical Writings*, and *Ethics: An Essay on the Understanding of Evil*, trans. Peter Hallward (London: Verso, 2000), pp. 80–87. It is worth noting that lately, Badiou has abandoned this doctrine, thinking it too compromised with a diffuse culpabilization of philosophy, and also has much reconfigured his theory of naming. See his forthcoming interview with Bruno Bosteels and Peter Hallward entitled "Beyond Formalisation" in *Angelaki* 8, no. 2 (2003): 115–36 .

Chapter 10

1. Following Dylan Evans, *An Introductory Dictionary of Lacanian Psychoanalysis*, (London: Routledge, 1996), pp. 59–61, I have translated the terms *fantasme* and *fantasmatique* respectively as "fantasy" and "fantasmatic." The term originates in Freud and is discussed at length by Lacan in the unpublished Seminar XIV (1966–1967), entitled *The Logic of Fantasy*.

M E R I D I A N

Crossing Aesthetics